Ride the Wind

The Andy Green Story

Sailor, Engineer, Entrepreneur

Joyce M. Green

Fulton Books, Inc.
Meadville, PA

Published by Fulton Books 2021

Every effort has been made to ensure the accuracy of this book. In the event you find any errors, know that it/they were unintentional. This is a biography, and as such, it is necessary to identify people and entities associated with the person who is the subject of this book. Some of you have been contacted prior to publication. Others are gone now, and it is therefore impossible to contact them. All those who were contacted were happy to be included in this book. It is my hope that this sentiment will be universal.

ISBN 978-1-64952-457-7 (paperback)
ISBN 978-1-63860-592-8 (hardcover)
ISBN 978-1-64952-458-4 (digital)

Printed in the United States of America

Andy Green sailing a PlasTrend Finn on Lake Worth,
Fort Worth, Texas (March 1963)

This book is dedicated
to all our friends
who have been with us
through the good times
and the bad times.
Some of you are mentioned
in this book; however, there are
many more of you. It would
be impossible to name all of you.
And it is also dedicated
to our grandchildren
that they may truly know us.

Ride

Andy and Joyce on The Bird, one of their fastest sailboats.

Andy and Joyce Green ~
Andy is showing a drawing of
the composite he designed for
Jim Halls grand prix race cars.

There is no way to condense Andy and Joyce Green's amazing life into a 2 page magazine article. The Port Arthur natives have shared an incredible love story, a passion for sailing and a constant quest for adventure. One of the first things you notice is that although they have done more in their "wiser" years than most 20 year olds and call many influential people friend – they are 100% genuine. First, you realize how much they are a partnership and how their personalities are a natural fit for their lifestyle. Andy says, "My bride was a natural partner, pretty, athletic, ready to walk on the edge. We met in church and jumped into marriage, moving out of town, and taking every risk as if it were a sure shot. I couldn't have made it without her." Joyce feels equally as strong about her husband and states, "I love adventure, and I do mean wild, exciting, even somewhat dangerous adventure; and the man I married certainly provided plenty of that! My idea of being a wife is also very unorthodox. I wanted to go everywhere with him and be his partner in everything he did."

Andy is a curious person and says he has been that way since childhood. This led him to pursue a career in civil engineering because as he states, "Challenge and performance anything (higher, faster, stronger) turns me on". This proud graduate of Lamar University met with one of the biggest challenges of his life when racing great Jim Hall asked him to redesign the chassis on a grand-prix race car. Facing the task head-on, the determined man finally developed an unheard of composite chassis model that would redefine the way all race cars are built.

the Wind

Roatan also is a little further south of our racing destination. It is a beautiful tropic isle at the foot of the second largest interior reef in the world.

CHAPARRAL

66

66

The Chaparral, one of the most famous Grand Prix race cars, was the first to be built with a successful composite unit-body chassis.

Andy proves that age does not have to slow you down... here he is part of the winning team that set a new course record at the 2002 Harvest Moon Race.

THE THRILL OF THE RACES
10:17:33

Another huge part of this action packed duo's life is sailing. Andy, a member of the 1968 Olympic Sailing team, is a true competitor noting, "My most memorable race was my first long distance ocean race (725 miles). We were not considered a competitor to be watched because we were the smallest boat in the 57 boat fleet. We were the overall winner and took all of the other prizes in the event. After a few more performances like that we changed the competitor's thinking. We were and are someone to be watched." Joyce even raised the family to love the sport. "Our family was somewhat like the pioneer families in that we all worked together and played together. Our two children (daughter, Terri and son, Lee) helped out in the business and we all sailed together. We all love the water (swimming, sailing, diving) and just about every home we have ever had has been on the water," she shares. They are not only masters at the sport – but even owned their own sailboat manufacturing company for a while. "One of the boats we built was the Flying Dutchman, one of the olympic classes, and it was my favorite boat. She is beautiful—sleek and fast and she has a trapeze. Her hull will come out of the water and skim along the top (plane). That is really exhilarating – quite a ride! "adds Joyce. The couple often sails by themselves to their second home in Roatan. The stories could go on forever and their adventure on the water is still going strong. For Andy and Joyce Green life is just too short to tread water. They would rather ride the wind wherever it leads.

Andy sailing the Flying Dutchmen with Atlanta Braves and media mogul Ted Turner.

By—Susan Simmons

Contents

Prologue

I was a child of the Great Depression of the 1930s. Cash was limited. This meant that to get the most out of every dollar, you had to carry every effort and project to the edge. The better you performed, the bigger the reward. Every structure was stiffer, stronger, and more rugged than the competition. I wanted everything we built to be the best. By satisfying those objectives, our products were in demand.

—Andy

Just dive in and think about the consequences later. That was how I lived my life from my earliest memories. My dad was a Pentecostal preacher, and I went along with him on every trip and at every opportunity, at least riding along with him until he left me with some of our friends.

I remember staying with the Muellers in Saint Louis. Clarence and Grace, the mom and dad, were members of Brother Ben Pemberton's church in Saint Louis. I stayed with them a lot. Plus, they had a son who was only sixteen days younger than me. His name was Bob, and he and I both loved excitement and adventure. I remember wearing his ice skates (with plenty of paper stuffed into the toes to make them "fit" me) over snow-filled yards and across streets (yes, he was dragging me) until we finally arrived at the frozen pond. I was thrilled! Even though I had never skated before, I tore out across the ice with my oversized skates. We spent that whole afternoon (before his worried parents finally found us), taking turns skating with our one pair of skates.

When Bob and I were both three years old, a little girl was born to the Muellers. They named her Joyce, after me, and so we called her "little Joyce." That name stuck, at least as far as Bob and I were concerned until long after she married and became a mother and even a grandmother!

I looked at everything in life as a great adventure. If we went swimming in the ocean, I wanted to go deeper and deeper (whether I could swim or not). When I rode the roller coaster, I always let go and put my hands up going down that first *big* dip.

Yes, everything was a big adventure as far as I was concerned. I had plenty of first cousins living in and around Port Arthur, where I grew up as an only child. Little did I dream of the thrilling adventure life had in store for me with the man of my dreams, Andy Green.

—Joyce

Chapter One

Joyce

We were married on November 9, 1954, about seven months before I finished high school. I had known Andy for about three years at that time. He was five years older than me, and had graduated from Lamar University in Beaumont with a BS in civil engineering that May.

We were attending the First Pentecostal Church in Port Arthur, Texas, where I participated in everything—playing the marimba with the band, singing in a girls' trio, plus active participation in all the activities of the church. Andy was somewhat more distant.

When I first met Andy, I thought he was very mysterious. He was about the only one of us who was going to college. He also didn't speak unless he had something really important to say. I, of course, talked with several of my girlfriends (and a few of the boys also) just about every day. Andy participated in all our young people's activities (and we had a large group of young people) like getting together, it seemed like every night at our youth group leader's house for volleyball (always at every get together) and other fun games like "clap-clap" and "gossip."

We also had beach fishing get-togethers, where we would drag a huge seine through the water and always caught a number of fish. Andy was a natural leader of these expeditions. I was the only girl who helped swim the seine out into deep water as Pentecostal girls did not wear bathing suits; so I just wore my street clothes (blouse and skirt). Turns out it would have been much more modest to wear a bathing suit as my skirt got torn almost up to my thigh.

I got engaged to my girlfriend's brother when I was just fifteen and in the tenth grade. He was eighteen. Somehow, I knew I would never marry this guy unless he went back and finished school. (He had quit when he was in the tenth grade.) Well, he did not. He joined the army instead and was sent to Germany after basic training.

Everything went well for a while until one night when Andy was taking me home after one of our young people's get-togethers. Only one or two of our group had autos, and so we would all pile in the cars for going and coming from these things. I shall never forget his words to me that night. I was the only one left with him in the car, and as he drove me home he said, "Joyce, I have a lethal affection for you." This literally blew me away! As I said, he only talked when he had something really important to say, and so I had no idea he felt this way about me.

Well, eventually I broke off my engagement to Arvin, and Andy and I began dating. We married when I was still seventeen (two weeks before my eighteenth birthday), and kept our marriage pretty much secret until I graduated seven months later.

I grew up in Port Arthur, Texas, where I was born, with plenty of cousins and friends. The Second World War started (for the United States) on December 7, 1941, with the Japanese surprise attack at Pearl Harbor. Since I was only five at the time, I had very little idea what was happening. Since then, I have learned how our nation came together as one to fight (and win) that war. As the Japanese Admiral Yamamoto said after the Pearl Harbor attack: "I fear all we have done is awaken a sleeping giant—and fill him with a terrible resolve."

All the young men wanted to fight in that war, and the recruiting stations had all they could handle. Women took jobs in our manufacturing plants, making tanks, ships, and guns. The adults bought war bonds and willingly underwent rationing. There were also plenty of "victory gardens."

My own dad (a Pentecostal preacher) went to work for Kaiser Shipyard in California, building "Liberty Ships". I was pretty much unaware of any of this; however, when mom and I went to join dad in California, we took the train (the Sunset Limited). It took us five days to get there, and the train was packed with soldiers—young men going to ship out from various ports in California. I had a ball! These soldiers would put me on their shoulders and take me to buy candy and ice cream at every stop. When the train was en route, we would all tell each other "little moron" jokes. Now I see that this was these young men's last taste of home, and I'm sure many of them never returned. I'm just glad this little five-year-old girl (it was 1942) was there to give them some happiness before their grim taste of war.

We were only in California for six months while dad was employed by Kaiser. I remember we lived in a motel among other families, most with young children like me. There was a swimming pool there, and all of us kids were in it every day. One day I decided to walk across a grape field (I think it was grapes) barefooted. None of the plants offered much shade, and it was all hot sun in between plants, but I was determined. Somehow, I made it across; however I don't remember going back. (Maybe I waited until evening.)

We returned to Port Arthur, and dad had the Kaiser-Frazer automobile dealership. Guess he made that deal while he was working for Kaiser in California. They even had a small car called the "Henry J". I drove it to junior high one morning although I was too young to have a license.

When I was about eight, I saw an article in our weekly magazine. It was a picture of a young soldier stumbling onto a beach. Blood was pouring from him. The caption read, "This Soldier Never Saw a Jap and Never Shot One". I remember that picture very vividly to this day. I was horrified, and I wanted to *do* something to help him.

Well, eventually the war was over (1945). We had VE Day (Victory in Europe) in May and VJ Day (Victory in Japan) in September. I was still only eight years old and was only just beginning to become aware of the terrible cost of the war.

Dad sold the Kaiser-Frazer dealership and began selling used cars. In those days, no one had much money, at least no one that we knew. As I said, dad was a Pentecostal preacher; however, he had no church then. When I was about twelve or thirteen, dad bought some property in Port Arthur and built a Pentecostal church. He named it "The House of Prayer". As Jesus had said, "My house shall be called a House of Prayer." Dad deeded the church to the saints (members) of the church. Well, in about a year's time, those saints went latter rain and kicked dad out of "their" church.

That was the last church my dad ever built or pastored. He had built and pastored the First Pentecostal Church in Port Arthur in the early 1930s before he and my mom married in 1935. Dad continued to sell used cars in Port Arthur and to preach occasionally for several of his friends who would invite him to speak at their churches.

When I was almost sixteen years old, a little baby sister was born to our family. It was November 6, 1952, and I would turn sixteen on November 24. I was elated! She was born that morning, and when I learned of it, I just walked out of school, got in "my" car, and sped away to the hospital. A policeman stopped me; however, when I blurted out my mission, he ended up accompanying me to the hospital. However, only two and a half years later, when Joanie was only two and a half years old, I would be leaving Port Arthur with my husband, Andy, to live in Fort Worth. Even though we visited Joanie sometimes, she and I never really got to know each other.

My little sister

Joan Eileen Moore

First Pentecostal Church on Sixteenth Street (Gulfway
Drive) in Port Arthur, Texas, early 1930s.

This church was built by Rev. E. L. Moore in the early 1930s. This
picture is Brother Moore standing at the front door of the church.
The Sunday school bus is on the right. Zula "Reeves" Moore wrote
on the back of this picture: "This church was built in the early 1930s
before we got married in 1935. This is our honeymoon car. We married in church parsonage by Reverend and Mrs. Dillon."

Rev. E. L. (Ernest Lee) Moore, September 1934

Year 1937, Joyce and Bob Mueller

Joyce with Mama Reeve's glasses

Year 1938

Piano recital

Joyce in choir robe

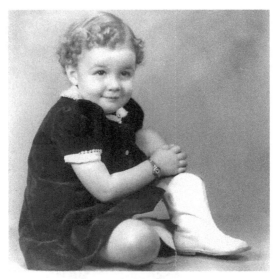

Joyce at about three years

Joyce at about ten

At the Pleasure Pier
Circa 1946

Patricia Moore's birthday party

February 1956
Two weeks ACDUTRA at Oxnard
In California

January 1946, age fourteen
Andy with his motorbike

Ada Beth McCord / Rosemary Avila / Barbara Ferguson
/ Patricia Moore / me / Margaret O'Brien
Campfire
Girls

Eloise Bean / Carolyn Vicknair / Patsy Moreau /
Beverly Poole / Marilyn Gower / Jane Redinger

February 1946
"Little" Joyce and Joyce

I'm having a ball!

Joyce with rabbit
Neil Thomas Salter

Joyce, eighteen years old

Chapter Two

Andy

Andrew "Andy" Green was born in 1931 in Santa Fe, New Mexico. It was only one year into the Great Depression, and millions of people were out of work. Soup kitchens were set up in some cities (like New York), and some people were given a meager amount of money (not enough to live on) from the government—for a while. President Roosevelt later established the CCC (Civilian Conservation Corps) to get the unemployed to work on government projects. Anyone who had a job in those days was lucky!

Andy's dad was one of the lucky ones. He worked for the Santa Fe railroad as a telegrapher, and they sent him to Los Cerrillos, New Mexico, to manage their station there. He often boasted that he "spoke" four different languages: English, French, Spanish, and "telegraphy". In fact, he was a very smart fellow, graduating valedictorian from his high school. It was there (in Los Cerrillos) that Andy's dad met and married his mom. She was postmistress for the Los Cerrillos Post Office. (By the way, Los Cerrillos was only about twelve miles south of Santa Fe, New Mexico).

Times were very hard all during the 1930s, even if you had a job. Andy's dad would "ignore" the pieces of coal that fell off the coal trains when they stopped at Los Cerrillos to allow scavengers to pick them up. He knew people were starving and cold, and he tried to help as best he could. He would even let people spend the night inside the station as it was warm there. Andy and his mom and dad lived in the station also, on the floor above the waiting room. The family left Los Cerrillos and moved back to Port Arthur when Andy was three years old.

At first, they had to stay with Andy's grandparents in Louisiana for a while. Then Andy's dad got a job as a laborer in the "bull gang" at the Texaco refinery in Port Arthur. He later became a journeyman / instrument man there, serving in that position until he retired. He refused promotion as he did not want any more responsibility. However, he did repair radios on the side. They also had two cows and sold milk and butter.

Los Cerrillos, New Mexico
(Circa 1930)

The Santa Fe railroad station is in the right foreground. Andy's dad worked as stationmaster here during the 1930s. He met and married Andy's mom here. (She was postmistress for Los Cerrillos.) They lived in the apartment over the station. Their son, Andrew, was born September 20, 1931, in nearby Santa Fe. The family left Los Cerrillos and returned to Texas when Andy was only three years old.
(Note: The railroad station is no longer there. It was purchased many years later by a family and moved to another town.)

Andy was a very enterprising young boy. He held various jobs while attending school. First, he delivered the newspaper on his bicycle (and later his motorcycle). He also delivered telegrams on his bicycle. He got a job at Rettig's Ice Cream shop on Sixteenth Street, serving up their delicious dishes. He also became the storeman (buying all the groceries) for Menhaden Fisheries purse boats. Now that was some job! The smell from those fish would permeate Port Arthur (even though the plant was some distance from town). However, they must have gotten used to it. Everybody slept and ate there, and Andy could not understand why people would cross the street to avoid him when he went to town! (The cooked Menhaden fish smell had permeated his pores!)

Andy always had his own money. He saved enough to buy his first motorbike, a Service Cycle that cost $241.03, brand new, including freight and shipping.

Andy also helped feed the family with his fishing while he was in high school. He and his friend, George (one of the Pentecostals) rigged up a trotline that ran across a channel in the Port Arthur reservoir (about 150 feet). They tied each end of the line to a rock and had hooks spaced every two feet along the line. Every evening, they would bait each hook with a small perch they had just caught that evening. Every morning, they would "run" the line to see what they had caught. They always had enough fish for both families, even though George's family was pretty large. One time, they caught a very large catfish (thirty-eight pounds). The two boys attached the fish to a pole that they carried between them and paraded their catch through the whole neighborhood! It was so big its tail drug the ground, even while suspended from their pole! George later wrote a story about their catch, which was published in *Boys Life* magazine. He titled it "That Summer".

Andy graduated high school (Thomas Jefferson) in 1950. He enrolled in Lamar Tech in Beaumont that fall. It had just become a four-year college the year before. Later, it became Lamar University. Of course, Andy paid his own way through college, working part-time at Sun Oil, Bryan Beck, and finally at Bethlehem Steel. In those days, a college education was very affordable (at least at Lamar Tech and similar state schools). It only cost $25 per semester, plus $15 for administrative fees for a total of $40 per *semester*! Four years would equal eight semesters or a total of $320! Of course, in those days, that was much more money than it is today because of today's inflation.

Andy

On his Service Cycle
with his dog "Spot"

With his little heifer

Ready to deliver
newspapers

With one of his catch

With a friend and
the Service Cycle

The happy
fisherman

Andy at seven or eight years old

Andy's degree was in civil engineering with a major in structural engineering. He said he pictured himself building roads and bridges through Africa. Later, he would end up building bridges right here in the United States although not the kind he envisioned then.

Andy was working for Bethlehem Steel in Beaumont when he graduated from Lamar in 1954. (He and Joyce married that November.) He helped to design the first offshore drilling rig, named "Mr. Gus". In those days, there were no calculators. Everything was done with slide rules. It took days to solve forty-four simultaneous equations (which they had to do in designing "Mr. Gus"). Now it can be done in a few seconds!

Now Andy decided he wanted to further his education by getting a master's degree in his profession: civil engineering. Convair, in Fort Worth (which later became General Dynamics), was offering to pay the cost of obtaining a higher degree for young engineers, so Andy applied for a job there, and they hired him.

In early 1955, Andy quit his job at Bethlehem Steel to go to work at General Dynamics in Fort Worth, where he planned to get his masters from SMU (Southern Methodist University).

He went to Fort Worth first as Joyce would not graduate until that May. The plan was to only stay in Fort Worth long enough to get his master's degree and then return to Port Arthur. Well, fate had other plans. About forty-four years later, Andy and Joyce did return to Port Arthur but not for long.

We believe God's hand has been at work in our lives from the beginning even though we did not realize it at the time. Looking back, you can see how He directed our path. For instance, Andy's work at General Dynamics positioned him to become an "expert" in the field of composites. This new material was looked down on by all the young engineers as there were no design allowables for it. They called the material "paint and bedsheets", and since the new young engineers are usually given the jobs nobody else wanted, that was the job given to Andy.

At first, Andy tried to use it like aluminum or steel, and he designed a small fairing that fit between the bomb pod and the B-58 airplane that carried the pod. His boss signed off on the part, and Andy proudly sent it to be fabricated. Well, it wasn't long before he got a call from the foreman in charge of fabrication, asking Andy to come down. When Andy got there, he saw two women attempting to fit this sticky glass fiber into the very small flanges Andy had designed for the part. Andy could see that the job was impossible. He told the foreman he would redesign the part.

Andy went to the library at General Dynamics and read everything they had on composites, and they had a very good library; however, there was still so much he didn't know. So he went to his boss and asked him how he (Andy) could learn about this material. His boss told him to visit every manufacturer in the United States, and attend every symposium on the material; in other words, learn all there was to know about this material. Thus, Andy learned about composites, and the knowledge he acquired became the basis for his engineering achievements. This was God at work in his life.

We bought our first house in Fort Worth shortly after I arrived there (in the fall of 1955). We first lived in a small rent house on Lake Worth. Now when I say small, I *mean* small! The bed (full-size) exactly fit in the bedroom, so you had to get in and out from the foot! The little house we bought in River Oaks in Fort Worth was like a dream to me. It had two bedrooms and one bath, a living room with a fireplace, a large dining room, a kitchen, and a breezeway, plus an attached one-car garage.

Our note for this house was $75 per month. We also had a $75 per month note on the '54 Ford Andy had bought just before we married. That was two notes for a total of $150 per month, and Andy only made $390 per month. Yet we were able to make the two notes, buy all our food, etc., *and* save $5,000 in three years! We did this by saving everything we could. Andy was in a carpool and only drove the car one day per week. I walked to the grocery store, which was only eight blocks away, and we limited our "night out" to one per month. It was always on dollar night at Underwood's Barbeque. (One serving of meat, and all you could eat of everything else.) We looked at it as a game. It was fun to see how much we could save.

We also had an old wooden "Snipe", a class sailboat that Andy had when we married. She was heavy, and Andy wanted to sail again—a fast boat. He knew she would never win any races, however we both sanded her until she had a really smooth bottom, and we sailed her in Lake Worth. Still, he had that itch...

It took three years for Andy to get his master's degree from SMU since he only went one night each week; however, he did get it. Joyce would ride with him to SMU in Dallas and wait in the car until he returned. She also did this while he went to his weekly Naval Reserve meeting in Fort Worth. He had joined the Naval Reserve when he was only seventeen as a seaman recruit and stayed in until his retirement in 1991 as LCDR. He was commander of the Reserve unit in Fort Worth.

Andy left General Dynamics in the summer of 1957 to try and start a business in Lampasas with a friend. So we sold that little dream home in Fort Worth and moved to Lampasas. I was pregnant with our first child. The new business did not work out, and so after four months, we went back to Port Arthur, our hometown. Andy thought maybe he might get a job there. He also wondered if he might go back to General Dynamics in Fort Worth.

By this time, we had a little baby girl. Terri Gale was born November 11, 1957, while we were living in Lampasas.

Our darling little Terri

It turned out GD did want him back. They offered him a job once again in Fort Worth, and that is where we went. By now, it was 1958. Andy was back at GD, and we had a new baby.

Andy got his masters in 1958, and we built a lovely brick home near Lake Worth that year. We had sold that Snipe in 1957.

One day, Andy read about the "Flying Dutchman" in one of his sailing magazines. This boat was one of the Olympic classes. She was twenty feet long and only weighed 276 pounds, "all up." (That is with mast, boom, sails, etc.—everything.) She is a two-person boat and has a trapeze. That is something the crew wears in order to get further out of the boat and help "hold her down" as she planes through the water. The skipper also has hiking straps, which enable him to hike out pretty far. Now this was Andy's kind of boat!

The article named the guy in Florida who had one of these boats, and Andy promptly called him, asking where he (Andy) could get one. The man knew of a group in Houston who sailed these boats. He gave Andy the name of one of them: Claude Cullinane. Well, Claude and the others in the Houston group became our life-long friends. Andy called Claude, and Claude invited Andy down.

Thus it was that Andy left our home in Fort Worth one Saturday to drive down to Houston to "see" these boats. Andy returned the next day pulling the *brand-new* Flying Dutchman that belonged to Fred Struben! (Claude's boat was too old for Andy to take a mold from.) Yes, this man they had never seen before had been entrusted with a brand-new Flying Dutchman (including trailer) to take to Fort Worth and possibly ruin trying to take a mold from it! Needless to say, we all became lifelong friends!

So here we are once again living in Fort Worth with Andy working for GD, and this time with a new baby girl, as well as the new Flying Dutchman Andy had brought back from Houston. We didn't realize it at the time, but this was the beginning of our business.

Andy at seventeen years old   LCDR Andy Green
Young seaman recruit in   Year 1971
the Naval Reserve

Andy Green, founder and president of PlasTrend and CTI
Year 1956

Summer of 1955
The Old Snipe: Andy (*above*) and Joyce (*below*)
work on the boat in the garage of their first little rent
house on Lake Worth in Fort Worth, Texas.

Chapter Three

The Chaparral and Early Years

Andy did take a mold from Fred Struben's Flying Dutchman, and the boat came through just fine. By the way, the name of Fred's Dutchman was "Our Hobby", and you could read that name on each one of the succeeding boats we built from that mold! From the mold, Andy took a hull.

So Andy now had a Flying Dutchman hull. That is only half a boat. You still need a deck and bulkheads, mast, boom, centerboard, rudder, etc., to name just a few things. He decided to build the deck from one-eighth-inch plywood, bending it over the spruce ribs he had made. It took him months to get that deck built. To me, it felt like a year, but he said it was only "a few" months. I began to look at the boat as the "other woman".

The mold on our porch   The spruce ribs for deck

We had the boat on a large covered porch at our home where he worked on it. Finally, Andy finished the deck of our new FD (Flying Dutchman), and we began to get her ready to sail. First, however, he took a mold of the deck. Now all we needed was the mast and boom, centerboard, rudder, wire rigging, sheets and lines, *sails*, trapeze, hiking straps, etc.

Here is the hull and deck finished and joined together.
Now for all the other things we needed to finish her.
(That is our friend Don Bean who helped us,
along with Andy and Joyce, all tired.)

It was about this time that one of the Houston group called and wanted an FD hull from our mold. This was Martin Bludworth, and he was a very good sailor, so, of course Andy said yes. Next, Claude Cullinane wanted a deck and a hull since his boat was so old. And then a group from the Chicago Yacht Club called and wanted five *boats*! We were in the boat business! It was 1959, and I was pregnant with our second child. Phillip Lee was born November 15, 1959, almost exactly two years after his sister, Terri.

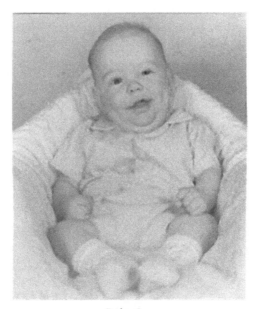

Baby Lee
(Two months old)

Andy fitting rudder on our first FD
Terri watching

Our mold we made for the hull

back porch at Oakridge

First FD, 1958–59

Don, Andy, Joyce

and the boat!

Our first FD, 1959

Walter Hopper with our first
Flying Dutchman, September 1960

We also got our first industrial job at this time. Clint Murcheson wanted six fiberglass honeycomb panels to use as skylights in his new home. We completed the panels, working out of our garage at our Oakridge home, and delivered them in early 1960.

We had also finished our first FD (Flying Dutchman) and began sailing her in 1960.

We joined the Lake Worth Sailing Club, which was near our home, and began sailing with them. It wasn't long until we had a fleet of Flying Dutchmen at the club, all built by us.

With all our boatbuilding business, we moved from our garage to a small shop in White Settlement, just outside the GD gates. This was a "moonlight" operation as Andy was working full-time for GD. It was 1961.

The Chaparral

In 1962, Andy was contacted by Hap Sharp and Jim Hall. They wanted a race car chassis and thought maybe this young engineer could build it for them; however, they did not tell Andy this. They were in the oil business (racing cars was a sideline for them) and told

Andy they were interested in small fiberglass buildings that could be used in the oil field. They were located in Midland, Texas, and Hap took Andy there to show him what they wanted.

Andy saw two side-by-side buildings with a racetrack behind them. Inside, they were full of all kinds of race cars and motorcycles, but nothing related to the oil industry. Andy was confused. Hap asked Andy if he would like to drive a race car. Andy said he was interested in boats, not cars.

Finally, they told him what they *really* wanted: a chassis for their race car! They planned to win the Grand Prix, something no US car or driver had ever done in fifty-plus years of racing despite many tries. Andy told them he knew nothing about designing and building cars, and they told him that was what they wanted: someone with no preconceived ideas.

Briggs Cunningham, America's Cup winner, as well as Lance Reventlow, the Woolworth heir, had both tried to build a car to win the Grand Prix. They failed. Now Lee Iococca, having just been made chairman of Ford, decided he would try. He purchased Lotus in England and had them design and build a car that they planned would be the first American car to win a Grand Prix Race. No one was paying much attention to Hall and Sharp in Midland, Texas. That turned out to be a *big* mistake.

Jim wanted a stiffer chassis as all the chassis then were metal space frames and were not nearly stiff enough. Andy asked how much stiffer he wanted the chassis, and Jim said he didn't know. Andy suggested, "How about four times stiffer"? Andy was young and full of confidence, and he figured he could do it. Jim said that sounded good to him. Jim said, "You don't have to have the fastest car, just the fastest average speed."

Then Jim asked Andy to sketch out on the blackboard there what he had in mind. Andy was caught completely off guard. His mind was racing as he walked up to that blackboard. The only thing he could think of was the bulkheading in the FD. This boat also had to be stiff as it was so light. So here is what Andy drew for them on that blackboard:

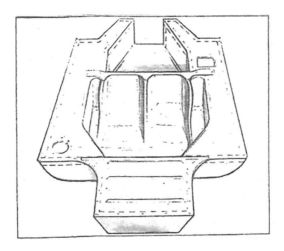

It was basically a Flying Dutchman cockpit, minus the bow and stern of the boat! Well, they seemed to like it. They told Andy they would let him know. About three months later, they told Andy to go ahead with the project.

Now we had very little money: only Andy's salary from GD. Still, Andy took the job, and they helped us get a loan from a Fort Worth bank. A few months later (in 1963), Andy quit his job at GD, and we sold our home and purchased a piece of property on the Jacksboro Highway. This property had a very large main building and had four apartments attached to it. We lived in one of the apartments and used one as our office. The two middle apartments were sometimes used as guest accommodations. We decided to name our new business "PlasTrend" to signify the plastic trend in the building industry.

We also had another industrial job (in addition to our boat building, which by this time also included Finns—another Olympic class—Tempests, a catamaran, and a small twenty-two foot keel/centerboard boat we named *The Mustang*). This other industrial job was a two-hundred-foot telescoping tower that we built for the Electro-Mechanics Company in Austin. The tower had to be built in forty-foot sections that would "nest" one inside the other in order to be transported on US highways. You see, this tower had to be portable to move from test site to test site. Its purpose was to determine the radiation spread from an atomic bomb. The US government had given the Electro-Mechanics company in Austin the job. Nothing like this had ever been done before, and a lot of people thought it would be impossible. Even in the company, there were cartoons of the tower in a "U" shape. Of course, Andy loved a challenge, and we completed and delivered this tower. Here is a picture of the tower erected on our property with Andy climbing it.

Telescoping tower for Electro-Mechanics Co., Austin, Texas

Merlin
Clint Murchison panels
Year 1960

Our first job

Terri takes a ride!

Honeycomb fiberglass panels for Clint Murchison house
Our first job!
Year 1960

Early 1960 Clint Muchison's panels

Another very interesting job we undertook at that time was one for the US government. It was building an early warning portable radar system to be used in the New Mexico desert. It was code named "RATSCAT", it was a Defense Early Warning System—a large portable structure supporting a sixty-foot diameter reflector for detecting and warning of enemy aircraft. Here are two pictures: one of it being fabricated in our shop, and one of it being erected in the New Mexico desert.

PlasTrend's Bruce Drebing works on "RATSCAT" project in our shop

"RATSCAT" project being erected in New Mexico desert

As for the Chaparral, it was an outstanding success. They *did* win the Grand Prix with it, as well as just about every other race all over the world. The Chaparral dominated the decade of the 1960s, and the unique chassis Andy designed for it changed the face of motor car racing forever.

There were a few bumps in the beginning, however. Hall and Sharp just had to trust this young engineer from Convair. They decided to go ahead with the chassis project, and so Andy began building the unique chassis in his shop on the Jacksboro Highway. Hall went to England to drive race cars for BRM (British Racing Motors) that year while Hap Sharp kept an eye on Andy.

Both Hall and Sharp knew that Andy's first love was racing sailboats, and they knew we were building them in our shop. So, Hap Sharp would arrive unannounced to see how we were doing on the chassis. There was a very long driveway to the shop, and everyone would quickly drop whatever they were doing to focus on the chassis. Hap was not fooled, and he finally had to get tough with Andy.

Also, Jim and Hap were working clandestinely with General Motors, and when Hap told GM they were having a unique new chassis built out of fiberglass by a young engineer in Fort Worth, they (GM) assumed the chassis would be the conventional "space frame" construction. The GM engineers told Hap that Andy was leading them down a primrose path. They said what he (Andy) was attempting was impossible. You see, they were limited by their concepts.

Hap called Andy, telling him what GM had said to him. Hap was very upset; however, we were about 85 percent finished with the chassis by that time, and Andy convinced Hap to go ahead. Jim was still in England, driving for British Racing Motors.

We finished the first Chaparral chassis, and Andy and I delivered it in a beat-up little pickup truck in 1963. It was a Sunday morning when we arrived with the chassis. Hap and Andy applied a torque test to determine its stiffness. (Remember, Andy had promised them that this new chassis would be "four times stiffer" than the old space frame.) Well, it was a little better than four times stiffer! Hap was so elated he called Maury Rose, a VP at GM, to tell him about it. He (Maury Rose) also was leery about believing it. He asked Hap about all their calculations to arrive at that stiffness, and Hap convinced him it had been done right. Hap also called Jim in England, and they decided to go ahead with two more of these chassis.

First Chaparral chassis delivered in 1963 by Andy
and Joyce in little beat-up pickup truck

Not long after that our shop in Fort Worth was visited by several GM engineers. They just came in, whether we liked it or not. Well, they made several trips, and sometime later Jim called and canceled the two additional chassis. Andy made one more trip to Midland, and now there were three buildings: Hap's building on one side, Jim's on the other, and a brand-new GM building in the center. The sign on the GM building read, "What you see here, what you hear here, *leave* here." Inside the GM building were several aluminum chassis for the Chaparral. They had plagiarized our fiberglass chassis! Jim asked Andy what he thought about these aluminum chassis. Andy said they would be stiffer; however, they would not be as tough.

Jim had a pretty serious accident sometime later. (This preceded the 1968 accident that ended his driving career.) In fact, he was in the hospital for a while, recuperating. Jim called Andy to come to Midland, and Andy figured we were about to be sued. (Jim had been driving the car with our chassis.)

It turned out Andy was all wrong. Jim now wanted Andy to go ahead with the additional chassis. Jim told Andy he (Andy) had been right about the aluminum chassis. Jim said even the mesquite alongside "Rattlesnake Raceway", their track in Midland, would crease the aluminum cars, and it was permanent. The fiberglass car, on the other hand, could really take a beating. It went through much worse than mesquite and never creased. In fact, the car Jim had been driving at the time of his wreck was now racing again.

The Chaparrals

The Chaparrals were the most innovative American racing cars. They broke more technical ground, advanced the high performance sciences farther, than any automobiles ever made there. They won races, they lost races, but more importantly they developed ideas. They pioneered new concepts in aerodynamics, in power units, in transmissions, in materials, and in testing procedures. (Quote from an article in *Cars in Profile* by Pete Lyons)

Three Chaparral 2 chassis were made by Green for Chaparral to race—two in wet lay—up epoxy resin and the last one, not delivered until 1964, in pre-preg phenolic resin. However, it has only recently become apparent that there was also a fourth chassis made, the evidence being displayed at the 1965 New York Motor Show when Hall's contemporary Chaparral 2 was displayed alongside a bare, unused tub at a time when three cars had been completed and had long since been out on the racetracks. Confronted with this in 1990, Hall replied enigmatically, "I guess there will always be these little Chaparral mysteries..." (Quote from *Chaparral, Complete History of Jim Hall's Race Cars 1961–1970* by Richard Falconer with Doug Nye)

Andy is proud to have contributed a major component to the development and success of the Chaparral. It was so revolutionary that forty years later, the Houston Chronicle ran a three-week Sunday issue recognizing Andy, Jim Hall, and Carroll Shelby for their work in advancing racing automobile performance.

Early 1960s
Original PlasTrend
9801 Jacksboro Highway
Fort Worth, Texas
(Next door to Vance Godbey's)

Wash on line
Our apartment home at PlasTrend

Year 1967 addition to PlasTrend

Andy climbing telescoping
tower, 1963

Chuck Carnes with section
of telescoping tower 1963

Joyce in the office (note
coat, it was cold)

Andy and Joyce in office 1963

Chuck Carnes and Skippy Wheeler, early 1960s

Keith Pratt, machinist, at Work

Ed Brawley

Ruth Carnes laying up a mold

Andy with Bud Upton, Production Manager

Andy at Jacksboro Highway Plant, February 1963

Dallas Boat Show, February 1964

Life in the shop
Sometime in the 1970s

Lee (totally bored!) on PT-30 no. 1 during a race

An Introduction to
PlasTrend

Builders of High-Strength Structural Reinforced Plastic Products
Chaparral Race Car Chassis
mid-1960s

Reprinted from the issue of August 16, 1963
PRODUCT
ENGINEERING
Copyright 1963 by McGraw-Hill, Inc.

Materials

DESIGN DIGEST

FRP

Structural solution

Take a plastic hog trough, put wheels under it and a 400-hp engine in it, and what have you got? If you're Jim Hall, Hap Sharp, and Andy Green of Texas you have a sports racing car good enough to win the US Road Racing Championship and the first car ever produced with a plastic chassis. When Hall and Sharp, of Chaparral Cars, Midland, Texas, decided to build their own cars they knew pretty well what they wanted.

One thing they were certain about before design started was the type of chassis they would use and what was expected of it. The complete frame was to be of stressed skin construction, weigh less than 150 lb, have a minimum axle-to-axle stiffness of 3000 ft-lb/deg and room for a 40-gal built-in fuel tank. The location of the seats, suspension pivots, engine, and transaxle mounts was dictated by size and suspension geometry. Working with a limited budget, Hall and Sharp decided on fiber-reinforced plastics and turned the job of developing a chassis to Green of PlasTread, Ft Worth.

Stiff problem. Toughest goal to achieve was the specified torsional rigidity—higher than any existing car —without exceeding the weight target, which was one of the lowest known. Design loads were based on a 3-g bump load—like hitting a curb at high speed—combined with a 1-g braking or cornering load and a safety factor of 1.5. Pure monocoque construction was impossible because of the large cockpit opening. The final solution was a series of torque boxes fused into a single irregular shape. A pair of torque boxes run down each side of the car and are connected at each end of the cockpit by bulkheads. The front bulkhead includes a torque box extending forward for suspension mounts and foot room. Stiffness of the torque boxes—proportional to the cross sec-

300 mph in a plastic hog trough

Combining chassis body, and gas tanks

tion area—was increased by making the outer skin the outside surface of the car and bringing the inner skin in to the driver's elbow and knee.

Since production is limited, open molds and hand layup with vacuum pressure bags is used with epoxy resins and woven glass cloth. Only the 14-in. tall inboard panel on the rear dogleg looked marginal when the stresses were computed—safety margin was a mere 0.03 in.—so hat-section stiffeners were added to prevent shear wrinkles. After the first car ran several races they were removed without causing difficulties.

Rivets and glue. The frame, consisting of 11 pieces, is assembled in a jig and pop-riveted together. At each point where a concentrated load is to be received—engine, suspension, or transmission—a suitable stainless steel bracket is riveted in place, then oil and water lines are installed. Additional layers of cloth and resin are applied at each bracket. After coating each joint with epoxy adhesive, rivets are used to provide clamping pressure and the entire assembly cured at 350 F for two hours.

After curing, rivets in the tank area are drilled out to prevent the rough ends from chafing the fuel bladders, and the frame is ready. Detail improvements during the construction of the first five frames have brought the weight down to 85 lb, and an accident has given graphic proof of the frame's ruggedness. Jim Hall went off the road and down a 30-ft bank at 80 mph, flipping the car end-over-end several times. All that broke was one corner of the frame—and Hall's left arm. The car was fixed in less than a week and won a 12-hr endurance race shortly after that. Hall's arm took a lot longer.

58

Chapter Four

Partnership with Ted Turner

Andy first met Ted Turner sometime in 1964. Oh, we certainly knew "of" him; however it was not until Andy delivered some FDs to our dealer in Atlanta, Georgia, that they really met.

Yes, Andy and I wore many hats in those early days, from boat deliveries, salesmen, bookkeepers, payroll clerks, purchasing agents, etc. At any rate, Andy was delivering these boats to Marietta, Georgia, as they were having a regatta there and Andy wanted to show the FDs. Ted Turner was there racing a Y-Flyer (small racing dinghy). Now Ted had also heard of Andy, having lost an automobile race in Florida to one of the Chaparrals just the month before and learning that Andy Green (whom he already knew built boats) had designed and built the chassis for the Chaparral.

Ted was fascinated by all this, and so he convinced Andy (along with the hitchhiker Andy had picked up) to sail his Y-Flyer and let Ted sail one of the FDs Andy had brought. Andy won in Ted's Y-Flyer, and Ted won in our FD, and that was the beginning of their association. Ted wanted to be partners with Andy in our boatbuilding operation, and he sent us a check to purchase a share of our business.

Andy never cashed the check until Ted called one day and asked him why he hadn't cashed the check. (It was for $50,000, quite a sum that we could certainly use.) At any rate, Andy explained to Ted that the boatbuilding business was not something he would want to be in. We were barely making it. We took no salaries ourselves and lived off Andy's Naval Reserve pay, which was not much. Well, the more Andy told Ted how bad the boat business was, the more Ted wanted in. Finally, Ted convinced Andy to let him become a partner with us in our business.

By 1967 Andy merged his business with Ted's, and we became part of Turner Communications Corporation. Andy said he learned a lot from Ted about how to run a business. Ted was tireless, and he knew every facet of what was going on with Turner Communications. He and Andy often traveled together as they were now sailing and racing the FD together, and Ted studied statements and reports as they traveled.

Andy admired Ted's business expertise. Ted had purchased Rice Broadcasting a few years before. At the time Ted bought it, Rice Broadcasting was losing about 5 million dollars a year! Well, Ted moved in to Rice Broadcasting (literally, even sleeping there) and worked until he got it to a breakeven point. That took about two years, and most in the broadcast world were laughing at Ted. Still, Ted kept on until he had Rice Broadcasting making money. Ted then took the company (which was part of his) public, and it was a great success. Ted was relentless when he went after something, and he usually was successful.

Ted was the first one to have a twenty-four-hour news broadcast station. They also laughed at that, but Ted went on to make that a great success also.

Andy made his first SORC (Southern Ocean Racing circuit) with Ted in 1964 or '65. He also raced to Jamaica with Ted in 1965, and I joined Andy there. It was a great vacation for both Andy and me. We later made several trips like this with Ted, where he and Andy would race to some exotic port, and I would join them there.

Andy and Ted decided to try for the 1968 Olympics, which were to be held in Acapulco. They had been sailing together and racing the FD for some time now. We shipped a number of boats to Acapulco (including several FDs and some Finns), which were to be raced in the 1967 pre-Olympics. I joined them there, and I even got to sail in those pre-Olympic games on a 5.5 meter, one of the Olympic classes. What a thrill! There were sea snakes in Acapulco Bay that were deadly, so you certainly didn't want to capsize!

Andy Green and Ted Turner at FWBC
Became partners with Ted in 1966

Andy and Ted racing FD on Eagle Mountain Lake

Andy & Ted on Eagle Mountain Lake

Andy Green and Ted Turner Acapulco, 1967, Pre-Olympic
Games sailing a PlasTrend Flying Dutchman

Well, Ted and Andy were selected for the 1968 Olympics, however they ended up fouling out of three of the eight races and could no longer be considered. They hit a starting mark in one race, an intermediate mark in another race, and finally, another boat in yet another race. Ted was the skipper, so…

While we were in Acapulco in 1967, Andy talked with George O'Day about building the Soling. He (George O'Day) had the license to build the Soling in the US, and we would have to build it under license to him. They made a deal, and the Soling "plugs" arrived in our shop sometime later. By now, we were building the Flying Dutchman (we eventually built more than five hundred of them), Finn, Tempest, Mustang (a 22 foot racer/cruiser with a keel/centerboard), the 420, and the PT-40, a forty-foot racer/cruiser. As we got into building ocean going racing sailboats, we called them all "PT's". That, of course, stood for "Plas-Trend".

In 1968, Andy and I purchase property on Eagle Mountain Lake and remodel (perhaps completely remake would be a better term) an old cabin there. We finally were able to move out of our apartment at PlasTrend. This was the house our kids really grew up in. It was on Eagle Mountain Circle, and after we finished remodeling it, it had three bedrooms and two baths. Our bedroom and both of the baths were at one end; the kids' bedrooms were at the other end. In between was a big open area that we divided up into the kitchen, living room, and dining room. A large teak cabinet separated the living room from the kitchen. Guess we were some of the first to have an "open concept" living area! The house had only one entry door.

Also, in 1968 Joyce's mother and sister moved in with us in Fort Worth. My dad had died in 1964, and mom was having a hard time. This lasted three or four months until mom finally found a little house she liked in River Oaks. She stayed in that house for over thirty years.

In early 1969, Andy and I took a trip to South Africa. We had built a Flying Dutchman mold for a man in South Africa who was to build FDs under license to us. Well, they insisted that Andy come to oversee the first FD produced from that mold and of course, I had to go along. They paid for Andy's trip, but not for me. Andy told me I could have my choice of new floors (the cabin/house had concrete floors stained a dark wine color), or I could go with him to South Africa. Well, that was a no-brainer for me. Of course I chose the trip!

Also in 1969 Andy raced with Wally Keller on one of our PT 40s that Wally had purchased to Cozumel, Mexico. I joined Andy there, and we enjoyed another little vacation, returning by way of Chichen-Itzá.

By 1970, Andy had decided to get out of Turner Communications, and so he and Ted made an agreement for us to buy back our company, PlasTrend. Ted gave us very favorable terms. We were to purchase our company back in three installments, I believe, over several months.

Meanwhile, we began building a thirty-foot racer/cruiser by a young designer. We had many problems, both with his design and with the man himself. We launched the first one on Eagle Mountain Lake and took her sailing to "shake her down". There were many things wrong with her. First of all, the rudder was too small, and the boat got out of control if the wind was above ten to twelve knots. The boat was also designed to fit the new IOR (International Offshore Racing) rule, and the sails would not measure in. Also, the designer designed the boat to have the mast stepped on deck with an offset stanchion in the cabin (to take the weight of the mast). Structurally, there was no way this would work! At any rate, we eventually got all these problems resolved and built several of these PT-30s in the 1970s. She was a very successful boat.

It was nearing the end of the year, and we decided to accompany Wally Keller and his family to Cozumel for a Christmas vacation. Our two children went also, making a total of eight on Wally's PT-40. Little did we dream what was going to happen in Fort Worth a few days later, on Christmas Eve, while we were in Mexico having a great time with our children.

Flying Dutchman

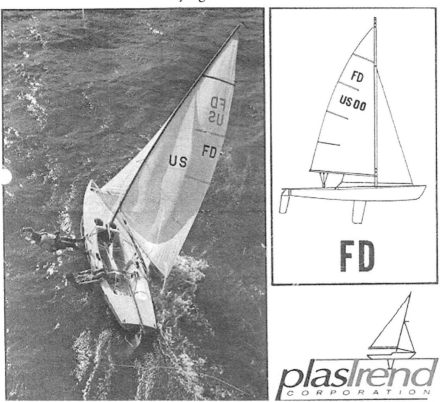

Finn

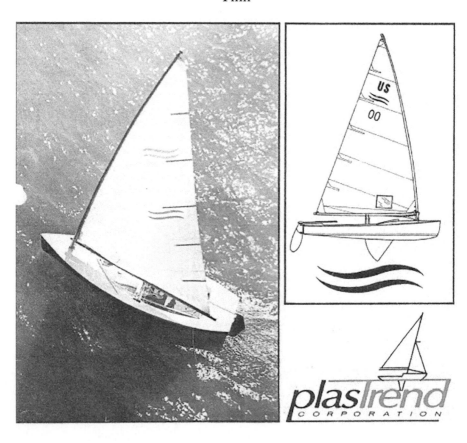

PT-22

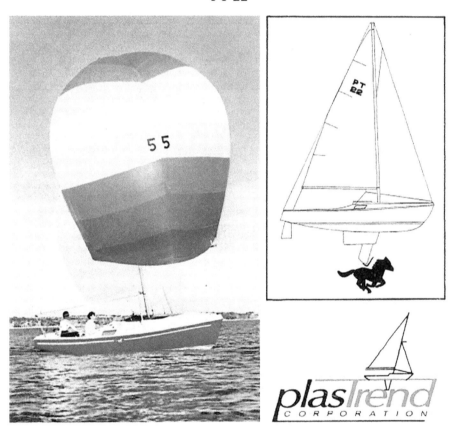

Check these features on standard boat:

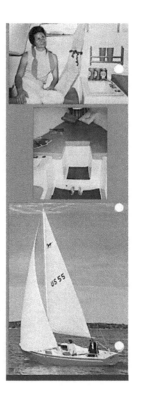

1. Seaworthy Construction
2. Hull and deck are fiberglass, taped together, making the hull and deck an integral unit
3. Flush deck for more lounging area
4. Keel-centerboard, 750 pounds of ballast
5. Anodized aluminum mast
6. Roller reefing round aluminum boom
7. Hinged mast step
8. Phenolic and stainless CB hoist
9. Stainless steel turnbuckles and standing rigging
10. Quality mariner blocks
11. Snubbing winches for jib
12. Three mooring cleats, two jib cleats
13. Jib track, twelve inches each side
14. Dacron main and jib sheets
15. Running lights
16. Battery box
17. Two large seat hatches
18. Fiberglass hatches and fashion board
19. Galley: sink, pump, and water tank
20. Coleman ice chest
21. Vinyl four-inch quarter berth cushions
22. Interior light
23. Full-width drapes separating the main and forward cabin
24. Step box—stowage
25. Plus main and jib sails

Join the aces...
Get on the PlasTrend factory team

Route 2, Box 935, Fort Worth, Texas, 76135, (817) 237-3327

PT-420

International Tempest

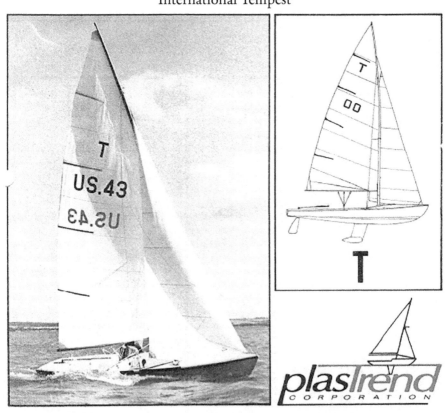

PT-40

Soling

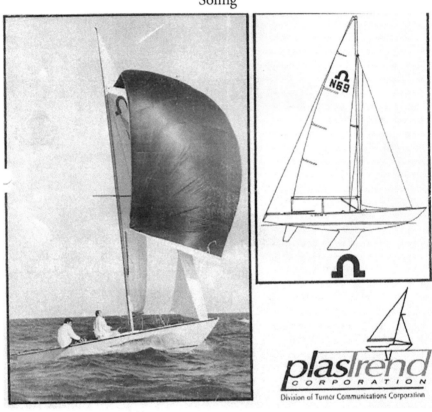

PlasTrend's PT-30
Same waterline length as a thirty-four footer at the price of a
thirty footer with the speed of a thirty-six footer a great boat!

Racer developed for the International Offshore Racing Rule

Ted Turner sailing PT-30 no. 1
(Andy in the cockpit, Skip Wheeler, and
Brittain Chance (designer) on board

The Achievement of Sailing Excellence

Chapter Five

Disaster! PlasTrend Burns
to the Ground

A disastrous fire was started by a boy (eleven years old) playing with firecrackers in our storage warehouse on Christmas Eve.

All of our molds were destroyed, along with all work in progress. We were under insured, and it looked pretty bleak. Our offices and records were untouched, as well as all hardware and some boats in the yard. All this while we were in process of buying back our company from Ted Turner.

Luckily, we had some good friends who worked with us to help us build back the company. Charlie Rogers (who had one of our PT-30s) loaned us his boat to take a new mold from. Ted Turner greatly reduced the amount we had agreed to pay him and gave us more slack on when payments would have to be made.

We also learned that we were "under insured" on our content insurance and would therefore have to pay 20 percent of the rebuilding costs. Skip Wheeler, who had our building insurance (and there was no "under insured" clause here), brought us a check for the building insurance very promptly.

Several of our vendors agreed to let us buy COD and pay off what we already owed them (at the time of the fire) as we sold the boats that were in inventory in the yard. Among these vendors were Jim Young (Riberglass), Mike Hopkins (PlasTex), and even Ian

Procter in England from whom we bought masts, etc. And there were many others who helped.

We would not have made it without their cooperation.

We also could no longer pay our employees. Bud Upton, production manager, came anyway, as well as Marvin Burkhalter, purchasing agent, and several others.

We are eternally grateful to all those who helped.

PlasTrend
Burned to the ground
This happened December 24, 1970

The fire was started by an eleven-year-old boy playing with firecrackers inside our shop. All molds and all work in progress was completely destroyed.

Lack of water contributed to the destruction. Fire trucks had to leave and be refilled with water before returning as there was no source of water there.

So here we are with a burned-down building, which included all of our boat molds and all work in progress, virtually no money and under insured. It looked like things could not get any worse. However, we were to find out a few years later that they could.

Some people urged us to declare bankruptcy, but we declined. We were all alive and healthy, and we had a number of boats in the yard that had not been touched by the fire. Our hardware and rigging building was separate from the main building and that had also been spared. Just about all our vendors were willing to work with us on a COD basis for new purchases while we repaid what we owed them at the time of the fire little by little as each boat in inventory was sold. We did this through means of a lockbox that the bank controlled.

All of the boats in our yard were Mustangs. There were about fifteen of them. How did we come to have unsold boats in inventory? We can only conclude it was God at work in our lives again. We had never built any boat on speculation; however, we did with these little twenty-two-foot Mustangs. Within that year (1971), we did sell all of these boats, paid off our vendors, and regained our thirty-day credit status with each of them.

Meanwhile, we wanted to rebuild PlasTrend. We finally got the meager amount owed us from our content insurance, and we had already received the money on our building insurance immediately after the fire. Now we went to the officials at the city to get our permit to rebuild. They said *no*. Even though we were on a major highway with only businesses in our vicinity, they told us our area was zoned commercial, not industrial. We thought we would be "grandfathered" in, that is allowed to rebuild since that is what we had before. They would not budge. What a dilemma!

Well, we were determined to rebuild our business, somehow, and so we began looking at other properties. This time we made sure any property we looked at was zoned "industrial". We also wanted to make sure there would be plenty of water on whatever property we purchased. You see, one reason our fire had destroyed everything in our main building was because there was no source of water there. The fire trucks came filled with water; however it soon ran out, and each one had to go and get refilled. Meanwhile, the fire burned on.

Our next-door neighbor, Vance Godbey, had a large swimming pool, and he agreed to let them use water from it; however, it just wasn't enough. We were in Mexico with our children then, completely unaware of what was happening to our company.

We would have to sell our present property in order to purchase anything else. Perhaps our next-door neighbor, Vance Godbey (who had a very nice smorgasbord restaurant), might be a candidate to buy our property. It turned out he was very interested, and he did buy the property. Andy was complaining to him about our fire one day, and he (Vance Godbey) told Andy that we would not know what tragedy was until or unless we lost a child, as he had done. This was a very sobering thought; however we could not imagine anything like that ever happening to us. We were to find out differently just a few years later.

We did find a nice piece of industrial property in Blue Mound just off Loop 820 in Fort Worth, and we bought it. Of course there were twenty-one owners, and each one had to sign off on the purchase. That took some time as one of the owners worked out of the country and was very difficult to reach. At any rate, the purchase was finally completed. Now all we had to do was build a building, move everything to the new location, and begin again. By now it was late in 1971. By this time, Andy was widely recognized as one of the foremost experts in the field of composites—a pioneer. This helped us tremendously in rebuilding our business.

Chapter Six

Starting Over

We purchased a steel building and had it erected on our new property. We built offices in the front of the building, upstairs and down. We also purchased a fire hydrant and had it placed in front of the building, to one side. That's right; we *purchased* a fire hydrant as, by now, we knew the value of having one close by.

There was a business in Dallas for whom we had been doing some work. We had been building radomes for them, and they wanted more. Well, we were barely there and not able to continue our work for them, and so they made an agreement with us whereby we became part of their company, DanRay, Inc. This way, we continued building their radomes, and they helped us financially.

Of course we continued building boats. We had a new PT-30 mold, thanks to our friend Charlie Rogers, and we built several more of these. We also began to get into offshore racing. We had built ourselves a PT-30 that we named *Phoenix* (up from the ashes). We entered her in the 1972 Vera Cruz Race, a race from Galveston to Vera Cruz, Mexico, some seven hundred miles away. We won that race, both class and overall. We had also entered three of the TORC (Texas Ocean Racing Circuit) races that year. People were beginning to pay attention to these boats!

By 1973 we had recovered enough that we were able to disengage from DanRay and "go it alone". We also began moving into the industrial business and away from boatbuilding. We also changed the name of our business to Composite Technology, Inc. as the name "PlasTrend" was too closely associated with boatbuilding.

That is not to say that we were no longer building boats however, as the boatbuilding business was just about all we had at that time. In fact, there was a designer in Massachusetts at that time who had designed a thirty-six-foot boat we liked. His name was Dick Carter. We made an agreement with him to build this boat. We called it the "Carter 36."

We were also still building the twenty-two foot Mustang (designed by Martin Bludworth), the PT-30 (designed by Brittain Chance), and the PT-40 (designed by Bob Derecktor). We only built three of these PT-40s. We also built a few "Peterson 34s" (designed, of course, by Doug Peterson).

Also, Gearhart-Owen, a close neighbor business, gave us the job of designing and building downhole wire line data gathering trucks. We built several hundred of these trucks for them. Another close neighbor, Ceramic Cooling Tower, gave us the job of designing and building a composite Cooling Tower, and they also became one of our major customers. These two companies gave us revenues until we developed our own product line of roofing, siding, and decking.

Meanwhile, our two children, Terri and Lee, were growing up. They both went to school in Azle, Texas (a few miles north of Fort Worth), and Terri graduated from Azle High School in 1976. We were all four working in the business, somewhat like pioneer families where everyone pitched in to work the farm or ranch.

Since Andy and I had to work at the business, Terri and Lee helped with the household chores. Both of them learned to cook and frequently cooked our meals. We called Lee the "king of the yard", meaning he was assigned to take care of it, and Terri the "queen of the house", for the same reason.

This was not to say that they had no leisure time. We lived on the shore of Eagle Mountain Lake and all four of us spent plenty of time on that lake. Terri and Lee spent a couple of summers at YMCA camp. Then they began attending Sailing Camp at the Fort Worth Boat Club, which was just about one-half mile across the lake.

They ended up spending five summers at Sailing Camp, even taking our dog, "Dog", with them. They had to take her as she would attempt to swim across the lake following them. Dog ended up being the only dog to not only attend sailing camp, but also being awarded a sailing award!

Terri and Lee sailed across to sailing camp in their little "Flying-Four–Temp-Finn". This was a 420 hull (yes, we were still building dinghies as well) with parts from various other boats added. She was actually a nice little boat. Sometimes the kids would cross the lake on Monday for sailing camp, and we wouldn't see them again until the next weekend.

Terri and Lee
(Year 1966 or 1967)

The Incomparable PT-32

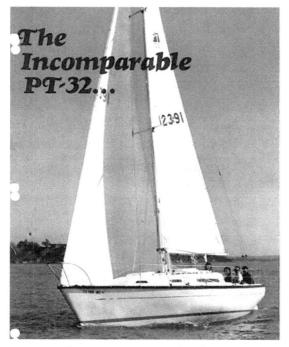

from Composite Technology

Several of their friends' families had cottages at the FWBC, and they would end up spending the whole week there. What an idyllic time for them!

Meanwhile, we built a Carter 36 for ourselves. We named her *Shazaam* (as in Captain Marvel when he would say "Shazaam" and turn into Captain Marvel). I fell in love with "Shazaam", and we ended up sailing her about ten thousand miles over the years. She was (and is) a great boat. I made a few of the races but more frequently helped Andy return the boat from Mexico after a race. Sometimes it was only Andy and me, and once or twice, it was all four of us.

I remember Terri remarked once when we were out in the middle of the ocean, "The only good thing about this is that everyone *thinks* you had a good time". She was so right. People who have not made an ocean passage don't realize you have to stand watches all through the day and night. You have to prepare your own food, and if there is rain or rough weather, you just endure it. There is no AC or heat, and the head ("bathroom") leaves much to be desired.

Shazaam was launched in 1974, barely in time for the Vera Cruz Race. We ended up aborting this race, as did most of the other entrees, as it was stormy weather for the entire race. *Shazaam* loved it. She is an ideal heavy weather boat; however, the crew, which included the man who built the plug for her hull (Tom Dreyfus), the sailmaker (John Rumsey of North Sails), the mast builder (Dennis Reigler), Andy, and our son, Lee, were just not up to it. After about two hundred miles, they dropped out of the race and returned home. Everyone on the boat had been seasick except Lee. However, when they decided to abandon the race and return to Galveston, everyone really came alive! They were singing and joking (and cooking and eating!)

Shazaam was not even complete when they started the race. There simply had not been enough time. Our son, Lee, was in the boat, working on it as she was being towed to Houston for the race. We hired an electrician to get her wired up as Andy could not be there until just before the race. When Andy saw the wiring job, he was appalled. Andy said, "This is the worst wiring job I have ever seen." The electrician said, "Right." One not-so-funny incident happened after they were back in Galveston. Tom Dreyfus, along with everyone else, had left to return to his home. Tom came back to the boat where only Andy and Lee were left. They were sleeping since everyone was very tired from the trip. Tom asked Andy if he (Andy) had any Vaseline. Andy was only half awake, but he directed Tom to the Vaseline. Tom pulled his pants down and began rubbing his entire bottom with Vaseline. Turned out he was burning up. Tom had chosen the storage locker for his clothes that also contained the battery. The battery had turned over and gotten battery acid all over Tom's clothes! Tom flew home to New Orleans, and he said by the time he got there, his pants were in shreds! John Mullen, another one of the crew, said when he heard the story, "And to think I coveted that storage bin."

The next year (1975), *Shazaam* was first overall in the TORC (Texas Ocean Racing Circuit). This was only the beginning of an illustrious racing record for *Shazaam*. In 1976, she was first overall in the Vera Cruz Race and second overall in the TORC. In 1977, she was third overall in the TORC; however, she came back to win the TORC AND the Vera Cruz Race in 1980. In 1985, she again won the TORC, as well as the Isla Mujeres Race, another race to Mexico.

Meanwhile, Terri graduated in 1976. She was working part-time for us at CTI, and she also worked for the FAA. She thought she might become an air traffic controller; however she decided to get a degree in accounting and work for our company. Andy planned to make her CEO (chief executive officer) or at least CFO (chief financial officer) of the company when she got her degree.

Lee graduated in 1978 from Ball High in Galveston. We had moved the boat business to Galveston in late 1976, shortly after Terri's graduation. Lee moved with us; however Terri remained in Fort Worth. We bought a little house in "Fish Village" in Galveston, so named because all the streets had fish names. We lived on Dolphin.

The boat business was named "Island Yacht Corporation". It was located on Teichman Road on Offats Bayou on a piece of property we leased from Rai Kelso. We later sold the boat business to our friend Marion Hayes, and we were thus, now completely out of the boatbuilding business. The year was 1977. (We had built the Peterson 34 in Galveston and had one that we sold in 1979.)

After graduating from Ball High, Lee worked for Rudy Teichman on a couple of his tug boats out of Galveston.

He said that was the hardest job he had ever had. He would come home all dirty and just dragging. He said he should have signed on as cook because the cook didn't have to stand a watch. Well, he didn't realize that the cook had many other duties. He had to buy all the groceries they would need for an entire week, bring them aboard and store them, and then cook three meals/day for all the hands, *plus* clean the dishes and galley after every meal, and have hot coffee *all* the time (plus snacks). If anyone needed some time off, it would be the cook!

In 1978 we were moving from our little Dolphin house to a new home we were building just off Teichman Road on Eighty-Ninth and one-half Street. Andy and I were riding our bikes from the Dolphin house to a storage building we had on the lot when Andy fell and broke his hip. This really threw a monkey wrench into our plans. Andy had to have surgery during which they put four bolts and nuts into his hip. (No one was doing hip replacement surgery in those days.) We had also planned to spend most of our time in Fort Worth (where our industrial business was located), and nothing could stop Andy from going to Fort Worth. Andy's doctor realized this, as did our friend Brenda Seawell, a physical therapist who would help Andy recuperate.

Brenda arrived in Port Arthur in a van she had rented. In the van, she had one of those reclining chairs that was completely adjustable, plus a one hundred-foot electrical cord to plug it in! Andy hobbled in on his crutches, got himself adjusted in the big recliner (we called it the "Java the Hut" recliner), and off he and Brenda went to Fort Worth.

Andy and Joyce aboard
Shazaam
in Vera Cruz, 1980

Lee and Mark Foster sailing Flying Dutchman in Spain, 1980

Phillip Lee Green
Selected for 1980 US
Olympic Team

Chapter Seven

Andy Green
Entrepreneur

Andy was by now being recognized nationally and internationally for his engineering accomplishments. Among his outstanding achievements are the following:

1. The chassis for the Chaparral race car (1960s).
2. Two-hundred-foot telescoping tower, portable on highway (1960s).
3. First competitive Flying Dutchman sailboat built of composite (1960s).
4. First long-span structural composite walkway bridges designed for clear spans to ninety feet (1974).
5. First FRP (fiberglass reinforced plastic) structural, corrosion-resistant roofing, and siding panels with lengths to sixty feet (1976).
6. First long-span FRP structural beams (1976).
7. Defense Early Warning (DEW) Line: Nuclear early warning system. Large portable structure supporting a sixty-foot diameter reflector capable of resisting wind loads to 125 miles per hour and detecting and warning of enemy aircraft (RATSCAT Project) (1960s).

8. First all-composite pre-engineered building system (including cladding, primary frames, girts, purlins, fasteners, doors, and vents [no metal]) (1985).

    Note: Three of these all-composite buildings were made, one for Apple Computer, one for AT&T, and one for Underwriters Laboratories. They had to be completely electromagnetically transparent and thus could contain no metal parts at all. An article by the Smithsonian about the Apple building was published by several newspapers. Also, articles about these buildings were in *Civil Engineering*, May 1985, including cover picture, and *Modern Metals*, and *Plastic Trends*, the same year.

9. All-composite unit body trucks for wireline operations in the petroleum industry (1970s and 1980s).
10. All-composite cooling towers.
11. First all-composite roofing and siding panels to pass Factory Mutual's corner fire test (1987).

JOYCE M. GREEN

Reshaping the Future

Cover of Civil Engineering
Largest engineering publication in the world

Fred Munoz, working on all-composite
CTI building

Reshaping the Future

John Casey (right)
Expounds to Andy and Glen Whitley, our accountant

Translucent TUFF-SPAN PANELS

City of Austin, Texas Installs 300,000 Square feet of TUFF-SPAN

Govalle Waste Water Treatment Facility

Largest FRP Panel Application

U.L. BUILDS TOTAL FRP STRUCTURE

TUFF-SPAN® composite materials include frames, purlins, panels, nuts, bolts, louvers and doors.

TUFF-SPAN® pre-engineered building installation at electronics test facility. TUFF-SPAN® components include rigid frames, columns, girts, purlins, cladding, and fasteners. All components were required to be non-conductive, non-magnetic advanced composites.

EXTRA! EXTRA! TUFF-SPAN Series FM Panels Pass Factory Mutual Fire Test... Now FM Approved

Gearhart-Owen wireline service unit

Factory Mutual fire test

Testing roof beam
Bud Upton and customer on beam (with lead pigs)

Tuff-span Tips

BULLETIN NO. 1

Virginia Galvanizing Replaces Chopped Strand Panels with TUFF-SPAN

Tuff-span Solves H.C.L. Problem for Dow Chemical

Dow Chemical Believes in the **Tuff-Span** FRP Wall System

TUFF-SPAN insulated FRP wall system at Dow.

TUFF-SPAN roof purlins installation at chemical plant. Chemical exposure is hydrochloric acid. This application of TUFF-SPAN beams which replaced steel was completed in 1980.

Tuff-Span Roof Deck Goes Up At Corn Refinery

Galvanizer Installs Tuff-Span Roof Over Hot Dip Operation

U.S. Government Installs TUFF-SPAN® Series 100

The first application for TUFF-SPAN® Series 100 was an 80,000 square foot siding installation at the U.S. Army Depot in Sacramento, California. To furnish this amount of composite siding for the first application of a product is similar to a rookie baseball player hitting a home run on his first at bat in the majors.

TUFF-SPAN® Siding Installation

-85-

TUFF-SPAN girts, purlins, roofing and siding panels replace failed coated metal materials at Axle

94

TUFF-SPAN® Advanced Composite Roof Decks

Beyond Steel Deck . . . . . Beyond Concrete Deck

TUFF-SPAN® roof deck is the only continuous glass, reinforced composite roof deck to go beyond conventional roofing materials--beyond steel, beyond concrete.

TUFF-SPAN® provides exceptional structural strength and stiffness with light weight and corrosion resistance.

Versatility For Built-Up Or Single-Ply

TUFF-SPAN® roof decks are developed for structural roofs in corrosive or non-metallic atmospheres. TUFF-SPAN® roof decks are similar in profile and depth to conventional metal decks and are extremely versatile in their support of both built-up roofs and single-ply roofs.

Structural Performance

TUFF-SPAN® is manufactured by a proprietary process developed by Composite Technology, Inc.®, in which straight, and continuous glass fibers oriented in the direction of the load are combined with specially formulated fire-retardant and corrosion-resistant resins.

TUFF-SPAN® roof decks have been listed for U.L. uplift requirements and are also strong enough to be used as a diaphragm to resist horizontal load.

New or Replacement Applications

TUFF-SPAN® roof decks are ideally suited for new or replacement applications. Older facilities can extend their service life with a new TUFF-SPAN® roof deck and single-ply membrane without replacing the existing built-up roof. The extreme light weight of TUFF-SPAN® will relieve stress on fatigued structural supports.

TUFF-SPAN® is also designed for high performance under exceptionally humid conditions such as in paper mills. The advanced composition of TUFF-SPAN® makes it superior replacement for asbestos T decks and concrete channel slabs.

Corrosion Resistance

The TUFF-SPAN® system simply will not corrode. The resin system in TUFF-SPAN® resists industrial chemicals and gases, humidity, chlorine, and other severe atmospheric conditions. TUFF-SPAN's® superior features provide a longer service life with quality performance than conventional materials. TUFF-SPAN® has a flame spread rating of less than 25 when tested in accordance with ASTM E-84. U.L. approved.

Easy Installation

Because of their light weight, TUFF-SPAN® roof deck panels are easy to handle and require less labor and fewer attachments for speedier installation.

-96-

95

JOYCE M. GREEN

FABRICATOR FOCUS

CTI Builds Future With FRP

For two decades, Composite Technology, Inc. (CTI), Fort Worth, Texas, has been a leader in the development and fabrication of high-performance fiber-reinforced plastic (FRP) composites.

Until 1971, CTI was known as Plastrend. That name, according to president Andy Green, reflected the company's commitment to the expansion and development of FRP applications, especially in the building industry.

It was, in fact, a new FRP venture that provided the impetus for this company's beginning. In the early 1960s, Plastrend received funding to design and manufacture the chassis and body for the first all-FRP race car. That effort culminated in the 1965 Chaparral automobile. And today, more than 20 years later, Green says CTI is again doing structural testing and evaluations with FRP composites for a major domestic auto maker.

One of CTI's most recent products is the world's first all-FRP pre-engineered building, fabricated for the Apple Computer Company, Cupertino, California.

Located in Pescadero, California, this 36' x 60' structure is used as a testing facility for Apple personal computers. All the wall and roofing panels, columns, beams and fasteners are constructed from FRP. Most of them were fabricated with DERAKANE 530 Vinyl Ester Resin, according to Green.

"The vinyl ester resin acts as a binder in the composite, giving the building superior structural integrity," he says.

FRP was ideal for this application because of its transparency to electromagnetic waves. During testing of computers, the building must allow the undistorted measurement of electromagnetic emissions, per FCC regulations. According to Tom Toler, sales manager for CTI, "While composites made with vinyl ester are non-conductive, it is their high strength-to-weight ratio that made this all-FRP building possible."

Another successful application for FRP in the building and construction market are "penthouses" — so named because they are built for the rooftops of metropolitan high rises (see photo). While no one lives in these penthouses, they do serve to conceal unsightly microwave reflectors and satellite dishes anchored to rooftops, while giving a complementary appearance to the structure. "Customized FRP structures are designed to look like the top of each building," Green explains.

Although many of CTI's projects are custom, the company has its own product line of FRP building materials, including cladding, purlins, girts and other ancillary items. Pulp and paper, chemical plants, mining, and wastewater treatment facilities are all major markets for CTI. Many customers in these industries buy fiberglass bridges — a CTI specialty.

Green says CTI lays claim to the longest clear span FRP bridge. Serving a loading facility for ships

An FRP penthouse (arrow) conceals a satellite dish atop a bank building. Note the similarity of the design of the penthouse with that of the building.

in Ft. Lauderdale, Florida, the 92' long, 4' wide walkway is designed to hold up under a load of 75 psf. He notes that these bridges are a popular item on his product roster, along with ladders and handrails. A major chemical company in Texas has had 56 FRP bridges in service since 1978, he notes.

Green says he has used DERAKANE to fabricate most of the bridges sold to date, and for more than half of his total vinyl ester resin jobs. He cites its long service life, strength, and corrosion resistance. "Because most of our projects require ignition resistance, we often use DERAKANE 530 Resin," Green says. Most of their production is continuous, yet CTI

(continued, Page 4)

Lubrizol Chemical Plant
Pasadena, Texas
Four seventy-foot CTI walkway bridges
installed in 1974–still there in 2020

Andy with Glen Whitley, our accountant, and
John Casey, office manager, 1983

Green
Courts the Edge

Sailor, inventor, and entrepreneur Andrew Green revolutionized racing worldwide with his design of the first all-composite racing car chassis—the immensely successful Chaparral—in 1965.

He credits much of his initial success as an engineer to the education he received at Lamar, where he earned a BS in civil engineering.

"I feel I received one of the best educations I could have received at the time," Green said. As a young engineer, he left his first job at Bethlehem Steel to move to General Dynamics in Fort Worth. "I was thrown in with engineers from A&M, MIT, etc., and I could stand on my own two feet. Lamar had something special, something a little different. At my commencement, Dr. Gray said if you learned nothing but how to think, then we accomplished what we set out to accomplish."

Andrew Green

Green learned how to think beyond established limits. Early in his career, the use of composite materials was not accepted because little was known of their performance, and no codes guiding their use existed. Green's vocation and avocation became one—to develop such a knowledge base. He began building high-performance boats for the Olympics, using new materials and gaining knowledge for other innovative applications.

Throughout his career, he has led technology innovation, often inventing methods and equipment to realize his vision—from structural design for offshore racing sailboats, unit-body trucks for wire line operations, automobile chassis and bridges with clear spans

greater than ninety feet, to cooling towers, and a proprietary composite structural system for industrial buildings.

He launched an industry built on composite technology, founding the Composite Center, Inc., to manufacture building materials for the chemical process industry. Traditional materials could not withstand the rigors of this hostile environment—one in which caustics, acids, and solvents are widely used. He developed a system to construct more resistant, longer-lasting buildings.

One material used to overcome structural stress was cement asbestos in which the cement was the binder and asbestos served as reinforcement. Later, companies were looking to replace asbestos because of its toxicity. Green met the challenge by creating a product called Tufspan. The venture enabled him to compete with the top companies, gaining recognition. W. R. Grace took notice and bought the successful company.

Currently, Green is chairman of the grant committee for Port Arthur's Economic Development Corporation and works to recruit companies to Port Arthur to boost employment.

As a Port Arthur native, his love of sailing began early and led him to sail on the US Olympic team, along with fellow crew member Ted Turner, in 1968. Green recently completed sea trials of a newly built high-performance ocean racing sailboat, christened *Bird*. The nine-thousand-pound, trimaran—the most recent of several racing boats he has built—carries one thousand square feet of sail and is built of carbon fiber, glass fiber, linear polyurethane foam, and epoxy resin. The next race is in October, and if Green has his way, he and his wife, Joyce, along with the rest of the crew, will be leading.

As with all ventures at the forefront of technology development, Green says, "You have to take things to the edge. You'll never know how close you are to success until you push the limits." This is an article from "Cardinal Cadence", a Lamar University Publication.

Yes, Andy has always "courted the edge", wanting to go higher, deeper, faster. He says, "You have to take things to the edge. You'll never know how close you are to success until you push the limits."

And so that is the way he (and I) have lived our lives. All I wanted was to be with him wherever he went.

We began the 1980s on a happy note. The four of us, Andy, Joyce, Terri, and Lee took a trip to Grand Cayman in the Cayman Islands in 1981. We swam and snorkeled and sailed and played games while we were there. We had begun this tradition of taking a family vacation each year some years before. Andy would give both Terri and Lee an assignment each year. Each of them had to write a treatise, saying where they would like to be in one year and where they would like to be in five years. This was to apply to them personally and to them in relation to our company. They grumbled some; however they knew it was good for them to take stock and to think about the future.

In 1982, the four of us took our yearly vacation at the end of the year. This time we went to Puerta Villarta, Mexico. Terri had found a house on Eagle Mountain Lake she wanted us to buy, and we entered into negotiations for it. Little did we dream this was to be our last family vacation…

December 1982
Here we are in Puerta Villlarta, Mexico
Terri, Joyce, Lee, and Andy

(This is the last picture of the four of us together. Terri was killed in an automobile accident in January 1983)

Chapter Eight

Tragedy

January 11, 1983, our daughter, Terri Gale Green, is killed in an automobile accident. Now we found out what real tragedy feels like. We could not function. Oh, Terri, our jewel!

Terri was an honor student at Texas Wesleyan University at the time of the accident. She was to graduate that May with a degree in accounting. (She had also graduated cum laude from Azle High School in 1976.)

We are so thankful to have had twenty-five years with Terri. She described herself as shy when she was sixteen years old; however she had drive and perseverance—plenty of it. She also believed in our company, passionately. At CTI, our employees would go to Terri with any problems they might have. She was a good listener. Our son, Lee, also took his problems to Terri, and she helped everyone, including him.

As I said, we could not function. Luckily, we had employees and many friends who helped us. Grey McGown (our lifelong friend who had worked for us briefly at one time) drove us to the funeral home to make the arrangements. I thought we should put off the funeral until those from out of town could be there; however Grey, who had come right into the director's office with us, said, "No, Joyce, you want to get this over with as soon as possible." He was right, and he had lost a four-year-old son himself, so he knew.

All our employees came to our rescue. Linda Bagley, in our front office, made it her business to notify all our business associates.

We were also in the middle of closing out the previous year (1982), and everyone helped with that. Terri herself (as if she had a premonition) had left notes, telling us what she had done and what still needed to be done. Condolences, cards, and food poured in. So many were there to help us, and we would not have made it without them.

Wesleyan honor student killed as car rams truck

A twenty-five-year-old honor student at Texas Wesleyan College was killed early Wednesday when the car she was driving rammed a truck stopped on the shoulder of Northwest Loop 820 to pick up three hitchhikers.

Terri Gale Green of 840 Sam Calloway Road was injured in the 1:45 a.m. accident at 2000 NE Loop 820 and died at 5:40 a.m. at John Peter Smith Hospital. A spokesman for the Tarrant County medical examiner's office said an autopsy showed that Ms. Green died of head and chest injuries. Police said a 1971 Chevrolet pickup stopped near the right lane to pick up three persons hitchhiking whose vehicle had run out of gas nearby. The truck driver and the hitchhikers were not seriously injured, police said.

The 1980 Dodge car Ms. Green was driving spun after it struck the rear of the truck, knocking it fifty feet from the road.

Terri had almost dropped accounting a couple of years before, however our accountant and friend, Glen Whitley, talked her into continuing. Jess and Brenda Seawell, our life-long friends, had also lost their son right after he graduated from high school. They helped us a lot. Also, LaRee Cruz had lost her teenage son a few months before this, and she also helped us. She said, "You *will* make it." It was surprising to learn how many had also lost

their children. Every call was comforting to us. We thank each one who helped us make it through this terrible time.

One final thought, about eight days before her fatal wreck, Terri told us about a dream she had that had really disturbed her. We were in process of buying a place on Eagle Mountain Lake, and Terri dreamed she was swimming in the lake at the foot of this property. She said she dreamed she saw a coffin sitting on the lawn there. She said she got out of the water and walked up to the coffin. It was open and she looked in. She said it was *her* in that coffin! I wonder, could she have been given a premonition?

Life was no longer sweet for us. We began to think about selling our business. The year 1983 had been a disastrous year for us in more ways than one. First was our daughter's death in January. On August 19 of 1983, Hurricane Alicia came ashore right through Galveston with 135-mile-per-hour winds. There was widespread damage, including some to our home. Then in December of that year, there was a devastating ice storm over the entire United States. Andy and I and Lee were in Jamaica at the time, still trying to hold on to some semblance of our past yearly family vacations. We returned to find frozen (and broken) pipes not only in Galveston, Houston, and Fort Worth but also in Chicago, where they are used to very cold weather.

Andy and I wanted to know if we would ever see Terri again. Yes, I had been raised in the Pentecostal church, and Andy was also involved in that church; however we had not been close to God since we had gotten so involved with our business. Yes, we attended church in Fort Worth for a while. Later, I attended a Baptist church close to our home on the lake.

In fact, I was rebaptized into that church and felt very guilty afterward. I had been baptized in Jesus' name when I was about twelve in Bro. Ben Pemberton's church in St. Louis. Now they baptized me in the name of the Father, Son, and Holy Ghost. I felt this was wrong. In fact, I did not become reconciled about this baptism until I talked with Ron Dart, our minister, friend, and mentor in the Church of God.

Meanwhile, life had to go on. When you have a business, you are forced to keep busy, and this was good for us. It helped us to keep our minds off our loss. Lee was also employed at CTI, and it was good for him as he and Terri had been very close.

Andy and I bought a fifty-foot sailboat in 1988. That's right, she was the first boat we owned that we did not build. We named her *Flank Speed* as she was very fast (for a monohull). She was first overall in the 1988 Galveston to Port Isabel Race, first overall in the 1989 Isla Mujeres Race, first overall in the 1990 Vera Cruz Race, first in class in the TORC Memorial Day Regatta, also in 1990. Then she won the TORC (eight races) in 1991. Quite a track record!

Lee married Cacy Cooper in October, 1989 in her hometown of Monahans, Texas. That is about eighty miles west of Midland. It was a big wedding with several showers, etc. They went on their honeymoon and returned to Fort Worth to live as Lee had his own business by that time. They had three children before divorcing in 1998. Eventually, Lee married again.

Lee's wedding
October 1989
Joyce, Andy, Cacy,
Lee and "Mama Green"
(Andy's mom)

Flank Speed
at start of TORC Race
Lee is steering
Jack Horton is trimming

AH for a life on the sea
Andy and Joyce aboard
Flank Speed
Returning from Merida, Yucatan, to Galveston, June, 1989

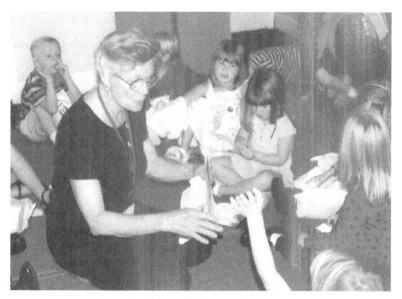

Feast of Tabernacles
Joyce teaching three- to five-year-olds, 1980s

Feast of Tabernacles
Beginner's class, (1980s)

Feast of Tabernacles
Beginners class

Chapter Nine

Our Return to God

We bought every version of the Bible we could find: King James, New King James, Living Bible, New International Version, etc. We wanted to know if we would ever see Terri again, or was this life all there was. Even though we had been taught that the dead are in heaven (at least most of them) and that they could "see" us, we really wanted to know. We asked every minister we knew, of every denomination, just what happens when you die.

We found that none of them really knew.

I had even bought a *Reader's Digest* version of the Bible, which I read all the way through.

I didn't really understand it, especially about sacrifices. We prayed and even watched ministers on TV. Both Andy and I would dream of visits from Terri; however that's all they were: just dreams.

One of the ministers we saw on TV said, "Don't believe me. Look it up in your own Bible." Well, we did, and sure enough, what he had said really *was* in the Bible! He was Herbert W. Armstrong, and there was literature we could get. We got it, and eventually, both Andy and I took a Bible correspondence course from the Church of God.

We learned some profound truths. The dead are asleep (not in heaven watching us); in fact, the Bible does not promise heaven (it promises land—the Promised Land, Beulah Land, etc.), and we learned that the seventh Day is the Sabbath Day, the day God blessed and hallowed when He finished His creation. It is the day God commands us to keep holy (the fourth commandment). We learned about God's Holy Days (which He commands us to keep) as opposed to these fake "holy" days as set up by man.

Also, we learned that we indeed *will* see our daughter again, along with many other loved ones, at the first resurrection. We began attending the Church of God, International in Fort Worth, and we visited the Church of God, International in Tyler. It was there that we talked with Ron Dart and Garner Ted Armstrong, and I became satisfied with my second baptism.

Now I felt that I had a duty to share the truths I had learned with my fellow man. So I wrote letters to Pat Robertson at the Christian Broadcasting Network, Marilyn Hickey at Marilyn Hickey Ministries, the Good Samaritans, and Coral Ridge Ministries. I also tried to share with some of our employees this newfound knowledge. I remember taking our encyclopedia to CTI to show a couple of my fellow employees what that encyclopedia said about Christmas. Well, I got a shock. They thought I was questioning their Christianity. I wasn't. I had just read what Isaiah said about lifting up your voice as a trumpet and telling God's people their sins. Boy, I was some zealot! Anyway, I found the scripture that says, "He that knows to do right and does it not; to him it is sin." I was relieved. These people were walking in all the light they had.

I also sent letters to everyone we knew, relatives and friends, letting them know that we would not be keeping Christmas anymore and enclosing an excerpt from our encyclopedia. Remember, I was always the one to "dive in and think about the consequences later". What I wanted them to know was that we would no longer be sending Christmas cards or gifts. I didn't want them to think we were snubbing them. Well, I got many responses, all of which were negative except two. At any rate, I later started sending out end-of-year cards, and most people now send us Christmas cards. That is just fine with me. I'm glad they still like me.

Chapter Ten

We Sell CTI

CTI was continuing to grow, however we no longer had the passion we formerly had for the business. Andy had intended to turn the business over to our daughter, Terri, after she received her accounting degree. Then, in January 1983, Terri was killed in an automobile accident. This changed everything.

Meanwhile, we continued sailing *Shazaam*, the Carter 36 we had built for ourselves in 1974. She was extremely successful throughout the remainder of the 1970s and all through the 1980s, winning the TORC (Texas Ocean Racing Circuit) several times, as well as several of the races to Mexico. The year 1987 was *Shazaam's* last hurrah with us. She won the Galveston to Tuxpan race, and one of our crew members (Anne Mullen) kept a log of the race, which we cherish. Only one other person ever wrote a log of one of our races or ocean passages, and that was Ron Dart, the Church of God Minister who was our great friend. We sold *Shazaam* later that year.

Year 1988: This was the year we sold our company to W. R. Grace. Andy and I flew to Boston, Massachusetts, to consummate the sale. All the due diligence had been done. The price had been agreed upon, and all inspections were complete. The broker we had hired (to find a buyer) accompanied us, as did our attorney, John McClane, who had been our attorney from the start of our business and remains our good friend today. He knew us well, having been through many legal ups and downs with us.

We entered the negotiating room; Andy and I, our attorney, John McClane, and two W. R. Grace representatives. On the table were several stacks of documents (one for each of us). Well, Andy and I had never signed anything without reading it first, except for one time when we borrowed $750,000 from TRIDA (Trinity River Industrial Development Authority). John had taken us out of the room then and told us, "It doesn't make any difference whether it says they are going to hang you in the morning. If you don't sign the agreement, you don't get the money." We went back in and signed *without* reading the document!

So we began reading the documents W. R. Grace had drawn up. Everything was as we had agreed except for one thing. We learned they (Grace) wanted us to accept full responsibility (liability) for everything we had ever built *and* everything that would be built in the future! Obviously, we couldn't do *that*! We may as well keep the company if we were going to be liable for all future products!

Well, negotiations went on for several hours, until around 11:30 p.m. when Andy stood up and said, "I feel like I am in a game with a bunch of card sharks, and I don't even know the rules." He told them that the deal was off and that we were returning to Fort Worth.

We returned to our hotel. We told John and the broker that the deal was off, and we were going home to Fort Worth. The broker couldn't believe it. He asked our attorney if we would really do it, and John told him yes, we certainly would. The next morning, as we prepared to leave, one of the W. R. Grace men called our attorney, John McClane. He asked John if we were really going to go home and call off the deal. John told him, "Yes." John told him that the three of us were leaving at that moment for the airport.

The W. R. Grace guy called us a day after we had returned home. He said they (Grace) would remove us from any future liability for products that would be made after they (Grace) had bought the company. He was actually crying. He said they had never had anyone do that before. At any rate, after they relieved us of any future liability, we went through with the sale.

Chapter Eleven

"First Passage" and Life
After Being in Business

We continued to sail *Flank Speed*, the fifty footer we had bought in 1988. She also was a very winning boat throughout the remainder of the 1980s and into the early 1990s, winning the TORC in 1991. We had a most enjoyable return home on *Flank Speed* in 1989. She had been first overall in the Isla Mujeres race, and Andy and I, along with several of our friends, sailed her home. Our friend and minister, Ron Dart, was one of those friends who made the return trip with us, and this was when he wrote his log of that trip. We cherish that remembrance. Here is his account of that trip:

"First Passage"
By
Ronald L. Dart
Merida, Yucatan to Galveston, Texas
June 18–22, 1989

Aboard:
Flank Speed

Crew:
Andy and Joyce Green
Steve and Vicki Brown
Charlie and Susie Rogers
Ron Dart

"Ron, I hate to disturb you, but you should come on deck and see this sky before the moon comes up."

It was Vicki Brown calling down the hatch. I was off watch and had found a remarkably cool and comfortable place to sleep. I was propped up among some sails under the forward hatch. (By this time, my standards of comfort had changed somewhat.)

I rolled out, slipped on my deck shoes, and worked my way aft. When I came on deck, the sky almost took my breath away. I had told Andy Green, the skipper of *Flank Speed*, that one of the things I was looking forward to was spending a night at sea, and this was exactly what I had hoped for. I had grown up in the Ozark Hills, far away from towns, where you could really see the stars. But even that sky had to take second place to the spectacular show of a clear moonless night sky at sea.

I had dreamed about doing this many times, but the only experience I had at sea was a hazy North Atlantic crossing on an ocean liner. I had read every one of C. S. Forester's Hornblower series—at least three times—and the works of several Hornblower clones. I had read about the days of fighting sail, the clipper trade, and had visited the Cutty Sark in Greenwich and HMS Victory in Portsmouth.

My experience with sailboats had been limited to two afternoon outings on yachts with experienced sailors. One in Australia, and the other off Galveston with Andy and Joyce Green. I still dreamed of going to sea although my appetite had been tempered somewhat by reading Francis Chichester's account of his record-setting, single-handed voyage around the world. While the romance remained, Chichester gave me a dose of reality.

In any case, my wife doesn't share my fascination and hates any boat that leans from the vertical, so I had pretty well written off the idea of making an ocean passage.

But then I met Andy and Joyce Green, experienced blue-water sailors and racers at that. When they invited me to meet them in Merida after the Galveston-Progresso Regatta and to sail back with them, I jumped at the chance.

So it was that I boarded a Continental Jet from Houston to Miami to Merida on Wednesday, June 14, to hook up with the Greens and the return crew, Charlie and Susie Rogers of Arlington, and Vicki and Steve Brown of Alvin—all experienced sailors.

We spent three days looking at the Mayan ruins at Uxmal and Chichen-Itzá and attended a couple of fiestas before our planned departure on Sunday morning.

As the time for embarking approached, I was not especially reassured. By Saturday night, out of thirty-three boats that had left Galveston for Progresso, only fifteen had arrived, and three of those were disabled—one lost its rudder, and two were dismasted. Eight boats were still not accounted for, and it was ten days after the beginning of the race before all of them were located. The race down had been very hard on boats and crews. The crew of the "Windswept" called the race, "The Eternal Beat from Hell." The one thing that puzzled me was how few of these expensive boats had reliable long-range communication. One of the boats was getting short on food and water before it was found by the Mexican Navy. Regatta planners might enjoy the help of some of the amateur radio clubs in their area when setting up communications. Hams are always looking for something useful to do with their toys.

Due to continuing thirty-knot winds and the time of year, tides were especially low. My first view of *Flank Speed* in Progresso harbor was not encouraging. She was sitting on her keel (a winged keel), and the front part of the hull was completely out of the water. Andy was afraid she was sitting on her rudder and was concerned about damage. I began to wonder about return flights to Houston.

A check of the tides revealed that we would have only one high tide that would give us enough water to leave. It would be slightly after 6:00 a.m. We couldn't afford to miss it, or we would be delayed twenty-four hours. I could see myself missing a Dallas to Los Angeles flight scheduled for Friday, but I was in for the deal.

We were all at the boat early with some of the experienced crew out in a borrowed dinghy trying to get the anchors up and the boat out of its mooring without running aground or fouling someone else's anchor line. I was trying to stay out of the way. Over the next few days, I was to learn that, on a sailing yacht, there is a fine line between trying to help and contributing to a disaster. This may be one of those areas where it is more dangerous to know a little than to know nothing at all.

By the published time for high tide, we were free and heading for the harbor entrance under diesel power, but we had no more than six inches of water under the keel. We also had a uniformed immigration official and an armed military policeman waving at us, and it was plain that they were not waving goodbye. It seems they wanted us to stop and clear immigration before leaving.

The skipper immediately faced two urgent questions. How deep was the water where they were directing us, and how long would it take to get out of there. We were not sure how long it would be before we were sitting on our keel again.

There was good news and bad news. The good news was that we still had five inches under the keel. The bad news was that the man who had to clear us would not be in until 0930.

It looked like one more night of Mexican hospitality was in the cards, but I underestimated Joyce. She bustled around, gathered up all the passports and paperwork, put on a big smile, and went inside to negotiate. I'm not sure how she did it, but without bribes or threats, she was able to talk the official into calling the man who had to clear us and getting his approval to let us sail. I had a feeling she had done this before.

Whatever the magic, we were underway again with at least two inches of water under the keel. We left the channel sailing due north out of Progresso with the wind just forward of the beam. It was beautiful sailing with seas running only two to three feet. We enjoyed a breakfast of eggs, sausage, toast, and coffee. Charlie Rogers muttered something about "killer weed".

As the morning progressed, the wind backed and strengthened to eighteen knots, and we spent the day beating to windward at about eight knots.

We arrived at Alacran reef at about 1700 hours. We spent some time looking for a convenient anchorage, hoping to do some snorkeling around the coral reefs. We finally anchored near another sailboat, and some of the crew tried out the fins and snorkels. Unfortunately, winds and currents made diving difficult.

After a cool swim, a sunset cocktail hour, and dinner in the cabin, there was some discussion about whether we would spend the night there at anchor or set sail to Galveston and spend the night taking advantage of the wind. The idea of a good night's sleep and the chance of better diving in the morning carried the day, so we set an anchor watch and spent the night. I got to enjoy a full moon on the 2300 to midnight watch, all the while taking bearings on the lighthouse to be sure we weren't dragging the anchor.

Monday, June 19, 0600: Overnight, the wind had veered to the southeast, but conditions had not improved for diving. It looked like our best course was to up anchor and head for home. The winds would be directly astern for Galveston. As we depart, Charlie notices more "killer weed".

As the morning drew on and the winds dropped, the skipper decided to change the Genoa for the big two-thousand-square-foot spinnaker. It made a difference of about one and a half to two knots. It may seem hardly worthwhile to a landlubber like me, but it represented a 25 percent increase in speed. In perspective, it could cut a day off what might have been a five-day journey. It was at this point I began to understand why sailors think in terms of miles per day instead of miles per hour.

After lunch, it began to get hot. I had been warned, so I was at least mentally prepared. Pretty soon, all of us who didn't have any specific duty at the moment were populating what shade we could find from the sail and studying the clouds to see when we could expect some relief.

Relief came in the form of a thundershower forming to the north-northwest. We saw it coming, and the crew started bringing down the spinnaker and preparing to set the jib.

Just as the spinnaker was stowed, the rain hit, and the jib was set in the rain.

Everyone's spirits soared after the rain—it was so much cooler. Even being wet was a pleasure. After the rain, we lost the wind for a quarter of an hour, but it returned from the northeast and freshened. The decision was made not to use the spinnaker for the time being, so the genoa was set instead. The wind increased to fifteen knots during supper, and a discussion ensued on the wisdom of dropping the genoa. It turned out that the wind moderated, so the sails were left as is. Charlie still seemed concerned about "killer weed".

The boat moved well all through the evening watch, but under a full moon and clear skies, the winds continued to veer and drop. I hit the bunk at midnight and began to concentrate on getting some rest. I was getting a little sleep between watches (we were running two hours on and four hours off. Being a novice, I stood watch with Andy and Joyce and was on from four to six and from ten to twelve on both circuits of the clock.) I hadn't known what to expect, except that I had been warned to get rest when I could. I couldn't sleep below in the afternoon—just too hot—so I relaxed and catnapped when I could. I have learned not to fret when I can't sleep but to simply rest the body, and it seemed to work. At first, the motion of the boat bothered me, but then I began to hum a few bars of "Rock-a-Bye Baby in the Treetop" and almost began to enjoy the motion. I rested well, but for the first couple of days at sea, I doubt that I actually slept more than one hour at a time. There were too many strange sounds, too much random motion.

Tuesday, June 20, 0730—breakfast is served. So far, so good. I haven't had a hint of seasickness although I get a little uncomfortable bending over below decks.

We had averaged seven and a half knots overnight, and the decision was made to put up the spinnaker when the morning watch came on.

In the forenoon, the wind died down to very light airs and left us with only three to four knots. Andy was continually making adjustments to keep us moving. By noon, it was dead calm. The anemometer turned once in thirty seconds. Somehow, the boat was still making one knot. *Flank Speed* is an ultralight boat built for racing, and she can make do with almost nothing—although I still am not sure how anything weighing eighteen thousand pounds can be an ultralight.

About noon, the skipper gave up, pulled down the spinnaker, and started the diesel. We motored for six hours, trading the peace and quiet for six knots. When we finally did get a breeze, the diesel was shut down (blessed quiet), and the spinnaker was set again. We were galloping along at four knots when the watch below (Vicki) surprised us with a delightful tequila and lime combination (fresh limes from the Yucatan, big and juicy) and canapés. Through supper, our speed increased to five knots, and by sunset, we were up to six knots. The beauty of *Flank Speed* is that she was doing this on a minimum of a breeze, so the swells were only one to two feet. It all contributed to a marvelous feeling of well-being. Only Charlie seemed to still be concerned about "killer weed".

It was beginning to cool down, and my new habit of grabbing rest when I could took hold.

I went down to catch some sleep on the sails under the forward hatch. I had been there long enough for it to get dark when I got the call from Vicki to come up on deck. I had forgotten how many stars a man could see on a dark night. We all stayed on deck just soaking it all in and naming the constellations. Then I heard a sigh from off to starboard—it couldn't have been ten feet away. It was a peculiar explosive sort of sigh. Then there was another to port and then another. A school of porpoises had joined us in the dark and were swimming alongside. I leaned over the side to look and for the first time in my life saw phosphorescence in the water.

This was followed by a startling display of heat lightning. I had heard of it, but this was the first time I had seen it. The dictionary says heat lightning is "vivid and extensive flashes of electric light without thunder seen near the horizon, especially at the close of a hot day and ascribed to far-off lightning reflected by high clouds." Maybe. It seemed to come from any point of the compass, and there was generally no source for the flash. It did not seem to come from the horizon. Only once did I seem to see a center for one of the flashes, and that was all. It was more like a strobe than lightning. There was no flickering, no lingering. It was there, and then it wasn't. I wondered what the first sailors ever to see it had thought. By all accounts, they were a superstitious lot anyway—even for the day.

We had one other phenomenon that night. From somewhere off the port bow, we heard a cry. All of us heard it, so it was no illusion. There were no seabirds in the area at all. A discussion ensued as to where the sound was coming from with someone thinking it was the rudder. We determined it was not. We heard it again, and I can only say that had I been on land, I would have sworn it was an owl. But I was right in the middle of the Gulf of Mexico, and the nearest land was two miles away—straight down.

To finish off the evening, the moon made a major production about rising, taking nearly an hour to work its way up and around a climbing cumulonimbus in the east, frequently peeking through the cloud to see how it was doing.

Andy allowed that the sailing that evening was the smoothest he had ever experienced.

I didn't want to miss anything, so I stayed up until my watch. When Charlie and Susie relieved us at midnight, I went below somewhat reluctantly. I stretched out and listened to the gurgle of water along the hull and heard Charlie and Susie harmonize "On Moonlight Bay." I went to sleep and slept four hours straight.

Wednesday, June 21: The wind had freshened through the night and continued to do so through the morning. Our speed was up, and we were occasionally surfing along at eleven knots. I kept on catnapping between watches and amazingly seemed to be getting enough rest. Everyone else must have been too because they were all in a good mood. Although Charlie was noticing more "killer weed".

Wednesday was a good day's sailing with everyone anticipating arriving in Galveston at noon on Thursday. We began seeing ships in the late afternoon—about 130 miles from Galveston.

Once again, we had tequila and lime at the happy hour, and this time, we had a floor show. A huge school of "wild and crazy" porpoises—the small, clownish variety—discovered us and called in all their cousins. We could see them coming down the sides of swells a hundred yards away in every direction. As they converged on the boat, curving around to the bow, they did all the "SeaWorld" jumps—one even did a somersault in the air. They stayed with us for nearly an hour, and the show went on the whole time.

We headed into another glorious evening with a breathtaking sunset. We had dinner on deck at about 7:30 p.m. with several thunderstorms lying across our wake in the distance. The first oil rig was in sight on the starboard bow.

Sometime in the early evening, Joyce blew Charlie's "killer weed" story. He was devastated. He was sure he had me nibbling on it and was all ready to set the hook by talking about killer weed coming over the side during the night and taking over human bodies. The after-dinner discussion was on "killer weed", "Fnarking" flamingos at the New Orleans Zoo (ask Steve Brown), and other snipe hunts.

This evening had a totally different feeling as we sailed into the offshore area. There were drilling rigs everywhere. They were pretty enough with all their lights, but somehow, I preferred the open sea.

As the evening wore on and the wind freshened, we began rolling hard in the following swells. It was wearing out the helmsmen. By midnight, it was plain that the spinnaker had to come down, so they did it in the dark and winged the jib out to port. With the sails better balanced, it was a lot easier on the helmsmen, and the rolling was not nearly so bad. It seems a wind directly astern is one of the most uncomfortable points of sailing for *Flank Speed*.

The morning watch was uneventful after a rough four hours of attempted rest.

Thursday, June 22, 0830: Landfall (or building fall), Joyce spots the twenty-one-story American National Insurance Building on the horizon.

We entered the channel before noon with the crew packing sails and putting away lines and sheets as we go. Everyone was up with new energy and the excitement of getting home.

When everything was secured and we had cleared customs, we had a few moments to share a beer and say our goodbyes. Everyone was tired, and it felt good to be home, but there was something about it…

When I finally got to my car and had some time alone, I reflected on what makes people go to sea. Long before the trip, Joyce had commented on how miserable they could be at sea, and yet… there was something that made them want to go back. I was lucky— very lucky. My first passage should probably go into the *Guinness Book of Records* as the easiest first passage a tyro ever had. I went to sea fully expecting to endure hardship. I suppose I had a little. It was hot. I didn't sleep much. There are no really comfortable places on a boat like *Flank Speed*. But this trip is a crown jewel in all the experiences of my life. And, as I told a friend, you cannot experience the middle of the Gulf of Mexico without going there, and you can't go there without some hardship.

Then there are the words of Charlie the Philosopher while we sat in the shade of the mainsail one afternoon, "Where else would two grown men like us sit still and discuss the development of a single cloud for twenty minutes." At sea, under sail, the simple things count."

Flank Speed—aground!

Flank Speed—interior

Captain Ron

Charlie in his element

Charlie Steering

Steve, preparing to hoist Main

JOYCE M. GREEN

Steve, getting help from Andy and Vicki

Steve, getting help from Charlie and Vicki

Joyce, "what fun we have"

Vicki

Steve

And the dolphins *all loving it*

Suzie: "Oh Lord, will
this ever end?"

"Just look at those thunderheads!"

Joyce amid lawn chairs and laundry

Ron, Charlie, and Vicki gathered in the shade

Joyce and Andy
Ah, for a life on the sea!

Now we began to welcome grandchildren! Lee and Cacy's first child, Phillip Lee, was born July 2, 1991. On January 29, 1993, their second son, Brandon Kyle, was born. Finally, August 2, 1994, their last child was born—a beautiful little girl named Lauren Elizabeth.

Andy and I were doing more traveling during those years. We visited Quito, Ecuador, and the Galapagos Islands in 1990. In 1991, we made a trip to Thailand, where we met a couple from Germany. We became friends with them, and they visited us in the US, and we visited them in Berlin sometime later.

In 1994, we made a trip to China with Lee. Lee was building some pultrusion machines at that time for a company in Beijing. Andy and I went on to Chengdu for a visit with some engineers with whom Andy had been corresponding. We returned home by way of Kuala Lampor, Malaysia, in May. We also bought our first trimaran—a small one which we named *Bird of Paradise*.

Meanwhile, we had begun attending the Church of God in Fort Worth in the late 1980s. We also began keeping God's Holy Days. I remember our first Feast of Tabernacles was in Branson, Missouri, where we shared a meeting place with country and western singers. That was okay as they came in as we were leaving; however we were staying in a motel just outside town, and the only road in was *two* lanes (one for traffic going, and one for traffic coming in)! It took us at least one hour to get to our meeting place each day. We were fit to be tied!

It is amazing that we ever went to another Feast. However, we did, and the next time we went to a Feast in Oklahoma. You see, there are Feasts of Tabernacles held all over the world. Well, we loved the one in Oklahoma and attended that one several times.

One of the most different Feasts we attended was one in Israel. In September 1994, we flew into Tel Aviv and went from there to Caesarea. We visited Mt. Carmel and Megiddo (valley of Armageddon [i.e., Har Meggido]). Then we visited Nazareth and the Galilee region, including the Sea of Galilee. I was surprised at how small it is. You can see across it.

We went to Jericho, Hebron, and Bethlehem. We even saw two people baptized in the Jordan River. We saw Qumran, Ein Gedi, and Masada (where the last Jewish Zealots committed suicide rather than surrender to the Romans). We saw the Temple Mount (where a muslim mosque now stands), the Mount of Olives, and the Garden of Gethsemene.

The last thing we visited was the Holocaust Museum in Jerusalem. There they document the mass murder of Jews during the Second World War. More than six million were murdered, most in Hitler's concentration camps. They also have a few graves just outside the museum to honor Jewish heroes of that war. Only one grave was a non-Jew. His name was Shindler, and he was a Nazi. He managed to save over nine hundred Jews from the gas chambers. To honor those dead, anyone may place a rock on that grave. Shindler's grave had far more than any of the other graves!

About two weeks after we returned home, there was a massacre at the Tel Aviv airport. We thank God we had gotten safely home. And we continue to attend the Feast of Tabernacles each year. The last few years have been in Destin and Fort Walton Beach, Florida. I taught the three- to five-year-olds for several years there and thoroughly enjoyed it.

In 1995, we left Fort Worth and moved back to our hometown of Port Arthur. We also had a house on Teichman Road in Galveston. In March, we visited our German friends in Berlin and came back through England where we visited our friend, John Davison.

Late in 1995, Andy got a hip prosthesis. That turned out to be quite some operation! Oh, the operation itself went all right; however, the medication they gave him to deaden the pain went to the wrong hip! He told me he thought he was going to die! In fact, I had gone home for the night, and he called me to come back. They could not give him any more medication, so he just had to suffer. Eventually, though, he did recover. He said never get any operation on a Friday if you have a choice. He had the second string in for the weekend.

Meanwhile, we built a house on Pleasure Island in Port Arthur during this time, moving in in December, 1996. We visited Guatamala in 1995. Then at the end of 1996 we took a trip to Honduras. This was an interesting trip and we ended up buying a (as yet un-built) condo in Parrot Tree Plantation on Roatan. We wondered if we were just sending our money into the wild blue yonder every time we made a payment on the condo. We finally got our condo, however not before hurricane "Mitch" devastated Honduras. This delayed construction on the condo, however we did not mind as most of the ships going to Honduras were taking aid for the people devastated by the storm.

By the way, we had been scheduled to return to the States via the ferry on which we had gone to Honduras (December 1996 to early 1997), however it never came. Their one ferry (on which they took people going and coming) had broken down on the way back down, and they ended up having to fly everyone back to the States. The ferry went bankrupt!

Now it was 1999, and we had a custom-built Dick Newick designed tri-maran built for us. We had her built in Brownsville and took delivery that fall and sailed her home to Port Arthur. (We had sold the smaller tri-maran the year before.) We named her "Bird".

Of course, we had to race "Bird". We entered her in the 2000 Vera Cruz Race, and she finished first by seventeen hours! Wow! Andy has always loved fast boats, and now he had the fastest! In 2002, Andy sailed the "Bird" in the Harvest Moon Race (from Galveston to Port Aransas). She broke the course record in that race, finishing in ten hours and seventeen minutes. (By the way, we held the previous record in the smaller "Bird of Paradise", which we had sold some time before). At this writing (2020), "Bird" still holds the course record. So Andy has held the course record for that race for over twenty years now, and counting.

We sailed "Bird" down to Roatan, Honduras in 2001, with our good friend John Levandowski. After about a month, we sailed "Bird" back to Port Arthur, Texas, with our friends John and Anne Mullen. (Anne had written the only other log of one of our ocean passages—an excellent account of our 1987 race from Galveston to Tuxpan, Mexico.)

Bird in Paradise
Roatan, Honduras

March 2001, left for Roatan / the trip home to the USA
(Beginning to see the Rigs) / April 27, 2001, arrived home

Painted by Joyce Green

Architect: Dick Newick
Built by Lone Star Multihulls
Built for Andy Green

Bird
Harvest Moon Regatta, 2002 Course Record
Galveston to Port Aransas, Texas, ten hours,
seventeen minutes, thirty-three seconds

Chapter Twelve

Easing into a Slower Lifestyle

Our son, Lee, married Jill White on November 24 (Joyce's birthday), 2003. Four years later (October 17, 2007), they have a beautiful little boy, Preston Miles. So here we are now with four grandchildren!

Andy will always be a boat lover, and as we began to slow down, he took up rowing, thanks to our friend John Mullen, a sailor and avid rower. (Joyce, who always follows Andy, also took up rowing.) Oh, we continued to sail, and over the next few years, we buy, race, and eventually sell several boats: a powerboat we had built in Roatan, named *Paya Princess*; a powerboat we named *Bayou Belle*, built in 2007; the "Blue Moon" a custom-built sailboat Andy owned jointly with his friend, Robbie Greene; and several other sailboats. We even bought a Pearson 26 in November 2012 and refurbished her. That was really a job. We named her "*Cinderella*" since we had literally brought her up from the ashes!

Our dear friend Claude Cullinane had died in 2005, and his widow asked us to get Claude's boat (a PT-30 named "*Toljaso*"), restore her, and sell her. We did this.

Meanwhile, we continued to travel (although we had slowed down some) and enjoy visits from friends and family frequently. Andy was also being recognized for his contributions and innovations in the engineering field. He was often called on to make speeches and/ or receive awards from universities and engineering organizations. Life was sweet in these our "golden" years. We had no idea that we were still to experience one more great tragedy.

We also continued our association with the Church of God. We attended the Feast of Tabernacles each year, in various locations, and I taught the little three- to five-year-olds. This was a lot of fun, as well as very enlightening.

One particularly memorable occasion was when I took our three grandchildren to Orlando, Florida, in July 2001. We went by train (the Sunset Limited), and we visited Disney's "Magic Kingdom" the first day, followed by "Gatorland", "Water Mania", "EPCOT Center", "Discovery Cove", and "Sea World", on each succeeding day. They had a ball! I, however, had quite a time watching over the three of them. I "preached" to them about not going off with any stranger, even if it was another child, etc. Here they are enjoying some of their adventures:

Kyle/Lauren/Phillip
at Gatorland with gator and snake!

Kyle/Joyce/Phillip/Lauren
fun at Splash Mountain

Getting ready to snorkel at Discovery Cove

Kyle and Phillip on the "Buzz Lightyear" ride
(Phillip's favorite)

Chapter Thirteen

Another Tragedy

2016: This year brought us tragedy for the second time. Our son, Lee, died on September 25. He had been ill for some time, suffering from diabetes and two strokes he had in September 2015

His right foot was amputated on August 24, and he died one month later from diabetes complications. He was living with us when he died. We had spent most of the year taking care of Lee. In this undertaking, we are most deeply grateful to our family of friends in the church. We could have never made it without them. There was Doug and Myra Garner, both RNs who helped unceasingly. There was Johnny and Liz Fore, who drove us to and from Fort Worth for Lee's funeral, as well as helping with countless other things. There was our dear friend Grey McGown in Fort Worth, who helped us plan the service (as he had done when our daughter, Terri, was killed in an automobile accident). There were so many friends who helped in so many ways, and we love and appreciate all of you. We know we will see Lee again in a much better place.

Some Final Thoughts

Bill Tinsley is a minister who writes a syndicated column each week for the paper. We never miss one of his columns. Some time back he wrote one titled: "Growing Old with God". We particularly like that one as we share some of his same thoughts about growing older. He said, "I am now a 'senior citizen.' How did this happen? I never intended to become one. I spent my life busy about making a living, raising kids, pursuing career goals, trying to serve God and others, and suddenly, I wake up and I am a 'senior citizen.' This was never my goal. I never looked down the corridors of time and wished that someday I could become a senior citizen." Ditto for us.

There are, however, several things about "maturity" that are good. If we put our minds to it we learn that (1) God is always there for us, and He will carry us when we cannot go it alone; (2) Never blame anyone but yourself when things go wrong; (3) Always tell the truth! (No matter how bad it hurts). You will find it is so much better than lying; (4) Learn to love and help others. This is very satisfying. "It is better to give than to receive"; (5) Use your time wisely. We only have so much of it, and we never know when it is about to run out.

Andy Green's motto: "Keep on keeping on"

Epilogue

Here Are Some of Andy Green's Unique Designs

Flying Dutchman: My first interest in building the FD (Flying Dutchman) came upon learning about the boat, then finding out that there were none available because the three builders in the USA (or those in Europe) were unable to build one light enough out of fiberglass to be competitive on the racecourse. I had a look at it and felt that with proper fiber orientation and skin support (ribs), we could build a fiberglass FD. We did, and Buddy Melges won a bronze medal at the Olympics in Japan with one of our FDs (PlasTrend/ Composite Technology).

Telescoping Tower: Dr. Fred Morris, president of Electro-Mechanics Company in Austin, Texas, had a contract with the US government that asked his company to provide them something that would be able to determine the amount of nuclear contamination resulting from nuclear blasts in the Pacific Ocean. It had to be light-weight and portable on the highway. We designed a two-hundred-foot telescoping tower (five forty-foot sections nesting one inside the other). This required absolute stiffness—no sag. We controlled and eliminated the sag in these tubes by means of an adjustable bar joist support for the mold.

Walkway Bridges: The coastal area has many chemical plants. These plants all have wastewater treatment ponds with large rotating agitators in the center of each pond. These agitators require periodic maintenance, thus requiring a bridge to the center of each pond. Most of these bridges were in the seventy-foot range. We manufactured one that was ninety feet long. These bridges must be capable of supporting a manned forklift. They were using steel bridges when they came to us. The steel bridges only lasted seven to eight years at the outside, even with periodic sandblasting and repainting. Also, these bridges had to be clear spans. We replaced the steel bridges with our fiberglass Tuff Span bridges. Our bridges were installed in many of these chemical plants, starting in 1974, and continuing through the 1970s. They are still there today—with *no* sandblasting or repainting!

Chemical Food Processing Plants: Have problems with corrosion to their steel cladding. Our fiberglass Tuff Span panels (some up to sixty feet) have solved their corrosion problems.

Cooling Towers: Some cooling towers have heavy ceramic tiles for fill and have a problem with the water (used for cooling) corroding the steel support beams. Our composite beams solve these problems.

All-Composite Buildings: PCs have to be shielded to keep microwaves from polluting the atmosphere. We designed and built three all-composite buildings: one for Apple, one for AT&T, and one for Underwriters Labs. There was absolutely *no* metal in any of these buildings from beams and girts right down to nuts and bolts. They had to be (and were) completely electromagnetically transparent.

Chaparral Chassis: Troutman and Barnes had designed and built the early Chaparrals. Now Hall and Sharp wanted to design and build their own. The primary feature for the design from me was a stiffer chassis. How much? I suggested four times stiffer. They said, "Okay, go for it." Their then-current chassis was 750 foot pounds per degree per wheel base. My goal was three thousand foot pounds per degree. We achieved this by using a completely different concept. We developed a totally new and revolutionary stressed skin chassis. Their race cars (and all cars up to that time) were using steel space frame chassis. This unique chassis revolutionized motor car racing.

Now about the Boats

"I have always loved boats and being on the water. That is one reason I joined the Navy when I was seventeen. So how did I come to build, as a business, the particular boats we built? Here is my thought process."

Flying Dutchman: This is one of the Olympic classes: a two-man twenty-foot centerboard boat that weighs only 276 pounds, all up. That is, with mast, boom, rigging, sails, etc. So first, I was attracted by her speed (she planes) and second by the challenge to build this boat in fiberglass (composites). The only successful FDs had been wooden boats when I built our first ones. The challenge was to build it that light (276 pounds) and yet stiff enough to hold her shape no matter the stress she was subjected to. We did build a very successful FD from composite. Buddy Melges was the bronze-medal winner in the 1972 Olympics on Sagayami Bay in Japan, sailing one of our FDs. Just about all of the top FD sailors had our boats. We built more than five hundred of these boats far more than any other builder.

Mustang: This is a twenty-two-foot bay boat. The designer, Martin Bludworth, had one of our FDs (he was one of the Houston group), and he knew we could build a light structurally sound boat. He asked me to build this boat he would design, and I said yes. Martin had another builder who had built all his other boats; however, this one was to be for Martin himself. He wanted one that would beat all the other twenty-two-foot boats and even up to twenty-six-foot boats. The Mustang ended up winning Yachting's "One of a Kind." This was a regatta (series of races) organized by *Yachting Magazine* to show once and for all which of the various boats in this size range was really the fastest. (Every builder advertised their boat as being the fastest.) This was a "put up or shut up" regatta. The regatta took place at the Chicago Yacht Club on the Great Lakes. The weather was fair, except for the last race which had strong breezes. The Mustang proved she was the fastest and the best, even without a "professional" crew. The big boat companies had Mallory Cup Champions skippering their boats. In our case, we had Andy, Joyce, and Mike Balma, our friend from near Chicago (who also owned one of our FDs).

PT-30: This is a thirty-foot oceangoing sailboat. It is the minimal size for going out on the ocean. She was designed by Brittain Chance and built by our company. She proved to be very fast, winning the Texas Ocean Racing Circuit several times, as well as many other regattas. Claude Cullinane (our friend and also the owner of one of our FDs, as well as a PT-30) said, "The PT-30 always goes five knots. It doesn't matter if the wind is blowing three knots or thirty knots". This is true, and it was in the lighter air that she really beat all the other boats.

Texas One Tonner: (Carter 36) This boat was designed by Dick Carter, and she was designed to fit the new International Offshore Racing Rule. It does not refer to weight (one ton) but rather to a formula that, when applied, would come out to two thousand. Our boats, called "Texas One Tonners", were winners. We owned one personally, and she was the "winningest" boat we ever had. She won the TORC three times, as well as numerous races to Mexico and many other series as well.

Peterson-34: This is a fast ocean-racing sailboat designed by Doug Peterson of San Diego. This boat also was a real winner.

About the Author

The author and her husband
November 9, 2019
Their 65th wedding anniversary

Joyce (Moore) Green was born in and grew up in Port Arthur, Texas. She is a "preacher's kid" in that her dad was a Pentecostal preacher. Some say that children of preachers (ministers) tend to be a little wild. If that means loving excitement and adventure, then that certainly describes Joyce.

She met her husband, Andy Green, in church, and they married in November 1954, a few months prior to her graduation from Thomas Jefferson High School in 1955. They have been together ever since; they celebrated their sixty-sixth wedding anniversary in November, 2020.

Andy and Joyce have been described as "soul mates" by some of their friends, and that title certainly fits. Joyce says she could never have imagined the excitement and adventure-filled life she has been blessed to share with Andy.

Lightning Source UK Ltd.
Milton Keynes UK
UKHW020656090123
415042UK00012B/1940